W9-BLU-087

Parents' Choice Approved

Parent Council® Selection

"The positive approach to child-rearing."
—*Cleveland Plain Dealer*

"A concise, effective book filled
with specific suggestions to help kids."
—*Education Today*

What Kids
Need to
Succeed

Revised,
Expanded,
Updated
Edition

*Based on a nationwide survey of over 100,000
young people in over 200 communities.*

What Kids
Need to
Succeed

Proven, Practical Ways
to Raise Good Kids

Peter L. Benson, Ph.D., Judy Galbraith, M.A., and Pamela Espeland

free spirit
PUBLiSHiNG®

Works
for kids®

Library of Congress Cataloging-in-Publication Data

Benson, Peter L.
    What kids need to succeed : proven, practical ways to raise good
  kids / Peter L. Benson, Judy Galbraith, and Pamela Espeland. —
  Rev., expanded, updated ed.
      p.   cm.
    "Based on a nationwide survey of 100,000 young people in over 200
  communities."
    Includes index.
    ISBN 1-57542-030-9 (pbk.)
    1. Child rearing–United States. 2. Parenting–United States. 3. Self-
esteem in children–United States. I. Galbraith, Judy. II. Espeland,
Pamela.
HQ769.B5118   1998
649'.1'0973–dc21
                            98–9850
                              CIP

What Kids Need to Succeed is based on *The Troubled Journey: A Portrait of
6th–12th Grade Youth* by Peter L. Benson, Ph.D., published in 1993 by
Search Institute and sponsored by RespecTeen, a national program of
Lutheran Brotherhood; on "The Asset Approach: Giving Kids What They
Need to Succeed," copyright © 1997 by Search Institute; and on other pub-
lications and continuing research by Search Institute.

Major support for Search Institute's work on developmental assets is provided by Thrivent Financial for Lutherans, a not-for-profit organization
providing financial services and community service opportunities for
Lutherans nationwide. Additional support is provided by the Colorado Trust,
Dewitt-Wallace Reader's Digest Fund, W.K. Kellogg Foundation, and others.

For more information about Search Institute, call toll-free 1-800-888-7828 or
visit the Web site at *www.search-institute.org*
For more information about RespecTeen, call toll-free 1-800-847-4836
or visit the Thrivent Financial for Lutherans Web site at *www.thrivent.com*

Index compiled by Theresa Wolner

20 19 18 17 16 15 14 13 12 11 10 9 8
Printed in the United States of America

Free Spirit Publishing Inc.
217 Fifth Avenue North, Suite 200
Minneapolis, MN 55401-1299
(612) 338-2068
1-800-735-7323
help4kids@freespirit.com
www.freespirit.com

Contents

What Do Kids Really Need?

Most adults today are deeply concerned about young people

We're worried about our own kids, our neighbors' kids, the students in our classrooms, the youth in our congregations, and kids in general. We've seen the stories and the appalling facts about teen pregnancy, violence, school failure, substance abuse, sexually transmitted diseases, eating disorders, and suicide. We've watched the news and stared at images of alienated, angry kids who seem unreachable and doomed. We feel powerless to help because nothing—no program, initiative, strategy, or organization—seems to be working long enough, hard enough, or for enough kids.

It's depressing, frustrating, and frightening, but it doesn't have to be that way.

What if you knew that there were specific, practical things you could do to make a tremendous difference in young people's lives? What if you saw documented proof that these specific, practical things really work?

The title of this book, *What Kids Need to Succeed*, is not an exaggeration. It's a simple statement of what you'll find here: powerful ideas for positive change.

1

These ideas can assure a better future for the young people you know personally, for all young people in your community, and ultimately for everyone—if you're willing to try them.

What kids really need are adults who care.

This book began with a series of community surveys across the country

From September, 1989, through March, 1990, students in grades 6 through 12 were given a 152-item inventory called "Profiles of Student Life: Attitudes and Behaviors." The inventory was developed by Search Institute, a non-profit organization based in Minneapolis, Minnesota, that specializes in research on children and youth. It was sponsored by RespecTeen, a national program of Lutheran Brotherhood, a nonprofit corporation that provides financial services and community service opportunities for Lutherans.

Over 46,000 students in 111 communities and 25 states took part in the initial survey. The results were published in 1990 by Lutheran Brotherhood and in 1993 by Search Institute as *The Troubled Journey: A Portrait of 6th–12th Grade Youth.*

Meanwhile, the survey continued and grew. Eventually more than 250,000 young people in 600 communities and 33 states—in small towns, suburbs, and big cities; in two-parent, single-parent, and adoptive families; in poverty, the middle class, and affluence—took the original Search Institute inventory. The first edition of *What Kids Need to Succeed,* published in 1994, was based on the results of that survey.

In 1996, the survey was revised and expanded to gather even more information about young people's lives. During the 1996–1997 school year, nearly 100,000 students in 213 communities and 25 states took the new survey. The facts and findings reported in this revised edition of *What Kids Need to Succeed* are based on the most up-to-date information available about students in grades 6 through 12 across the country.

The surveys revealed some amazing things

As Search Institute started analyzing the results of the surveys, we asked ourselves: Why do some kids grow up with ease, while others struggle? Why do some kids get involved in dangerous activities, while others spend their time contributing to society? Why do some youth "beat the odds" in difficult situations, while others get trapped? We recognized that many factors influence why some young people succeed in life and others have a harder time—including economic circumstances, genetics, and trauma. These factors seem difficult and even impossible to change, *but they aren't all that matters*. Our surveys revealed that the difference between troubled teens and those leading healthy, productive lives is strongly affected by the presence of what we call **developmental assets.**

The usual definition of assets is "property or resources." We chose this term because the things we identified—building blocks for human development—act like assets in a young person's life. They increase in value over time. They provide a sense of security. They are resources upon which a child can draw again and again. They help young people to make wise decisions, choose positive paths, and grow up competent, caring, and responsible. And they're cumulative, meaning that *the more assets a young person has, the better.*

We first identified 30, then 40 developmental assets— good things every young person needs in his or her life.

The first 20 are **external assets.** These are things in a young person's environment (home, school, and community) that support, nurture, and empower him or her, set boundaries and expectations, and make constructive use of his or her time. The external assets are:

SUPPORT

1. Family support
2. Positive family communication
3. Other adult relationships
4. Caring neighborhood
5. Caring school climate
6. Parent involvement in schooling

EMPOWERMENT

7. Community values youth
8. Youth as resources
9. Service to others
10. Safety

BOUNDARIES AND EXPECTATIONS

11. Family boundaries
12. School boundaries
13. Neighborhood boundaries
14. Adult role models
15. Positive peer influence
16. High expectations

CONSTRUCTIVE USE OF TIME

17. Creative activities
18. Youth programs
19. Religious community
20. Time at home

The next 20 are **internal assets**—attitudes, values, and competencies that belong in the head and heart of every child. The internal assets are:

COMMITMENT TO LEARNING

21. Achievement motivation
22. School engagement
23. Homework
24. Bonding to school
25. Reading for pleasure

POSITIVE VALUES

26. Caring
27. Equality and social justice
28. Integrity
29. Honesty
30. Responsibility
31. Restraint

SOCIAL COMPETENCIES

32. Planning and decision making
33. Interpersonal competence
34. Cultural competence

35. Resistance skills
36. Peaceful conflict resolution

POSITIVE IDENTITY

37. Personal power
38. Self-esteem
39. Sense of purpose
40. Positive view of personal future.

How many of these developmental assets do American kids have today? Although they should have at least 31, most have only 18—a start, but not nearly enough. Here's a graph of what we found:

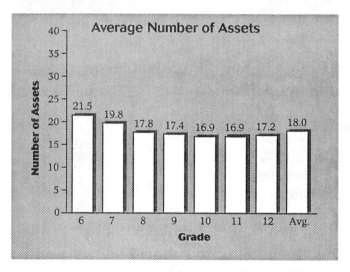

In general, older youth have fewer assets than younger youth. And boys have fewer assets (16.5) than girls (19.5). Here's another way of looking at how many assets young people have:

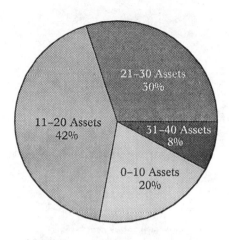

More assets mean
fewer problem behaviors

How do we know that the total number of assets makes a difference? When we looked for specific high-risk behaviors—behaviors that are known to potentially limit psychological, physical, or economic well-being during adolescence or adulthood—our survey revealed how powerful the assets really are. *Young people who have more assets are much less likely to get involved in these problem behaviors.* See for yourself.

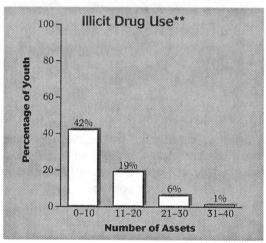

*Has used alcohol three or more times in the past 30 days or gotten drunk once or more in the past two weeks

**Used illicit drugs (cocaine, LSD, PCP or angel dust, heroin, and amphetamines) three or more times in the past 12 months

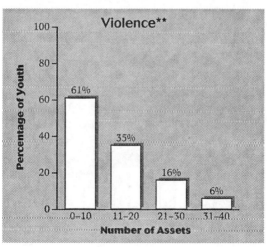

*Has had sexual intercourse three or more times in lifetime

**Has engaged in three or more acts of fighting, hitting, injuring a person, carrying a weapon, or threatening physical harm in the past 12 months

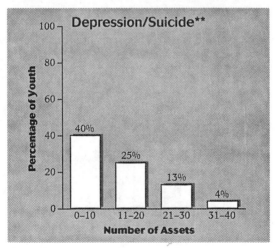

*Has skipped school two or more days in the last four weeks and/or has below a C average

**Is frequently depressed and/or has attempted suicide

More assets mean more positive behaviors

We also found that it works the other way—that young people who have more assets are much *more* likely to get involved in positive, thriving behaviors. Here's the evidence:

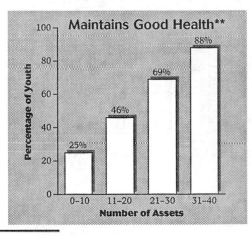

*Avoids doing things that are dangerous

**Pays attention to healthy nutrition and exercise

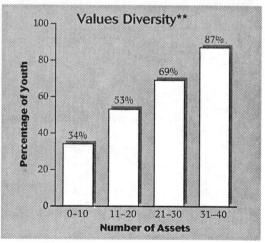

*Helps friends or neighbors one or more hours per week

**Places high importance on getting to know people of other racial/ethnic groups

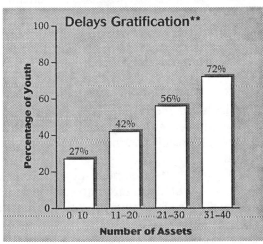

*Gets mostly A's on report card

**Saves money for something special rather than spending it all right away

You can be an asset builder

What Kids Need to Succeed describes the assets and gives you concrete, practical suggestions for building them in young people. As you can see from the list on pages 4–6, the assets aren't complicated. Most cost nothing in terms of money. Many are things you may already be doing. You won't find any radical, experimental, or theoretical ideas in this book. What you will find is a commonsense approach to raising good kids so they're free to grow into competent, contributing, responsible, compassionate adults.

In reality, there are probably dozens of other assets that are also important to helping young people succeed, but this list is a good beginning. If our kids could have many of these assets, we would all be a lot better off than we are today. As you start thinking seriously about asset building, you'll likely find many other ways to provide positive support for the young people in your life.

Not every idea you'll read about here will work for everyone. If you try an idea with a particular child or group and it doesn't work, don't stop there. Keep reading! We've included *more than 900 ideas* for families, schools, communities, and congregations. There's bound to be one that gets results . . . then another, and another, and another.

This book does not attempt to describe everything you need to know or do before implementing an idea. For example, if we suggest that you recruit adult volunteers into a school, community organization, or congregation, you'll need to ensure that appropriate systems are in place to provide a safe, enriching environment for everyone, both kids *and* adults.

Despite the best efforts of concerned and involved adults, not every young person will end up with all 40 assets firmly in place. But it's important to remember that *the more assets a young person has, the better*. This is not wishful thinking. It's a fact that is clearly supported by the survey results.

You can start today

Whether you're a parent, a teacher, a community or religious leader, or just an adult who wants to help kids, you can begin building assets today. This *positive* approach to youth development is not about crisis management, although young people who have these assets face fewer crises. It is not about stopping and preventing problems, although young people who have these assets face (and create) fewer problems. Instead, it's about investing wisely in our youth, increasing their exposure to positive, constructive activities, and instilling values and skills that will guide them from the inside.

Building assets is not a quick fix. It takes time and commitment from individuals and communities—caring adults. It's worth it *because it works*.

This book presents literally hundreds of practical ideas for parents, schools, communities, and congregations to try. We have kept them brief and to the point, because we mean this to be an action handbook, not a lengthy dissertation. You won't find step-by-step instructions or how-tos. You'll need to decide out how to shape the ideas to suit your particular circumstances. What resources are available to you? What programs and activities already exist? What other adults can help you? Get input from young people, too. What do they want and need? And how can they help?

In our experience, when people first learn about the assets and their power to change lives, they want to get started right away. Use this book as a jumping-off point.

Get together with your family, friends, and neighbors to plan ways to try these ideas in your community. Brainstorm your own ideas.

Throughout this book, you'll also find special sections called "Tips for Teens: Build Your Own Assets." Share these with the young people you know. You may want to start by telling them about the study and showing them the charts on pages 8–13. Most kids really want to stay out of trouble and succeed in life. When they understand how powerful the assets can be, they may decide to get involved in shaping their own future.

Here are six key points to keep in mind as you begin (and continue) to build assets:

1. **Everyone can build assets.** All adults, youth, and children can play a role. Building assets requires consistent messages across a community.

2. **All young people need assets.** While it's crucial to pay special attention to those youth who have the least (economically or emotionally), all young people can benefit from more assets than they have.

3. **Relationships are critical.** Strong relationships between adults and young people, young people and their peers, and teenagers and children are central to asset building.

4. **Asset building is an ongoing process.** It starts when a child is born and continues through high school and beyond.

5. **Consistent messages are important.** Young people need to receive consistent messages from their families, schools, communities, the media, and other sources about what's important and what's expected.

6. **Intentional redundancy is important.** Assets must be continually reinforced across the years and in all areas of a young person's life.

A few words about some of the words we use

We use the words *parents* and *parent* throughout this book to indicate children's primary caregivers. Of course, not all kids live with two biological parents or even one biological parent. Rather than spell out "biological parent, adoptive parent, step-parent, foster parent, grandparent, guardian, or whatever" each time we refer to a primary caregiver, we've opted for simplicity and brevity. If you're an adult who's raising and guiding a child, then when we say "parent," we mean you.

We use the word *congregation* to indicate the people you worship with and *place of worship* to indicate where you go. We have chosen these terms over "church," "temple," "synagogue," "mosque," "meeting house," and others that refer to specific faiths because we want to be sure to communicate the importance of asset building in *all* faith communities and traditions.

This book has been written for a broad, general audience. As you share the information and discuss the assets with others, we hope you will use the words that feel most comfortable to you.

Let us know how these ideas work for you

We'd love to hear your success stories, and we welcome your suggestions for building assets in youth. You may write to us at this address:

Free Spirit Publishing Inc.
217 Fifth Avenue North, Suite 200
Minneapolis, MN 55401-1299

Or send us email at:

help4kids@freespirit.com

It's our hope that building assets will become a nation-wide effort—that people in every community will work to create a better, more positive future for all children.

Let's get started.

> Peter L. Benson, Ph.D.
> Judy Galbraith, M.A.
> Pamela Espeland

Add Up Your Assets: Checklists for Kids and Parents

How many assets does your child already have?

The average young person we surveyed has 18 assets out of the 40 we identified. If you're a parent, you're probably wondering how many assets your child already has. The checklists that follow can help you find out.

The checklist on pages 21–23 is for kids and teens themselves; the one on pages 24–26 is for parents. Both are adaptations of the original Search Institute youth surveys.*

1. **Start by making photocopies of each checklist.** You may have more than one child, and you may want to return to the checklists later, after trying some of the suggestions in this book, so we recommend that you not write in the book itself.

---

* Please note that these checklists are not intended nor appropriate as scientific or accurate measurements of developmental assets. They are provided here to give you a starting point for discussion and awareness.

2. **Complete the checklists separately.** Have each person total her or his responses.

3. **Afterward, meet with your child to share and discuss your responses and perceptions.** Does your child report more or fewer assets than you expected? Do you and your child have different ideas about the assets that are present in your child's life? You may be surprised by something your child says. If so, try saying "I didn't know that! Tell me more. . . ." As you'll see, the checklists provide a great opportunity for conversation and discovery.

Parents and kids who have talked about the checklists have found this to be an enriching experience in and of itself. It's also an asset builder. When you take the time to talk seriously about the checklists, you're strengthening Asset #2: Positive Family Communication.

On each checklist, the numbers of the statements correspond to the numbers assigned to the assets. You may want to identify the assets that seem to be missing from your child's life, then turn immediately to the pages in this book that describe ways to build those assets.

A Checklist for Kids and Teens

Check each statement that is true for you.

- ❏ 1. I feel loved and supported in my family.
- ❏ 2. I can go to my parents or guardians for advice and support. I have frequent, in-depth conversations with them.
- ❏ 3. I know three or more other adults (besides my parents or guardians) that I can go to for advice and support.
- ❏ 4. My neighbors encourage and support me.
- ❏ 5. My school provides a caring, encouraging environment.
- ❏ 6. My parents or guardians help me succeed in school.
- ❏ 7. I feel valued by adults in my community.
- ❏ 8. I am given useful roles in my community.
- ❏ 9. I serve in my community one or more hours each week.
- ❏ 10. I feel safe at home, at school, and in my neighborhood.
- ❏ 11. My family has clear rules and consequences for my behavior, and they monitor my whereabouts.
- ❏ 12. My school has clear rules and consequences for behavior.
- ❏ 13. Neighbors take responsibility for monitoring my behavior.

❏ 14. My parents or guardians and other adults in my life model positive, responsible behavior.

❏ 15. My best friends model responsible behavior.

❏ 16. Both my parents or guardians and my teachers encourage me to do well.

❏ 17. I spend three or more hours each week in lessons or practice in music, theater, or other arts.

❏ 18. I spend three or more hours each week in school or community sports, clubs, or organizations.

❏ 19. I spend one or more hours each week in religious services or participating in spiritual activities.

❏ 20. I go out with friends "with nothing special to do" two or fewer nights each week.

❏ 21. I want to do well in school.

❏ 22. I like to learn new things.

❏ 23. I do an hour or more of homework each school day.

❏ 24. I care about my school.

❏ 25. I read for pleasure three or more hours each week.

❏ 26. I believe that it's really important to help other people.

❏ 27. I want to help promote equality and reduce world poverty and hunger.

❏ 28. I act on my convictions. I stand up for my beliefs.

❏ 29. I tell the truth—even when it's not easy.

❏ 30. I accept and take personal responsibility for my actions and decisions.

❏ 31. I believe that it's important not to be sexually active or to use alcohol or other drugs.

❏ 32. I'm good at planning ahead and making decisions.

❏ 33. I'm good at making and keeping friends.

❏ 34. I know and am comfortable with people of different cultural, racial, and/or ethnic backgrounds.

❏ 35. I resist negative peer pressure and avoid dangerous situations.

❏ 36. I try to resolve conflicts nonviolently.

❏ 37. I believe that I have control over many things that happen to me.

❏ 38. I feel good about myself.

❏ 39. I believe that my life has a purpose.

❏ 40. I'm optimistic about my future.

A Checklist for Parents

Check each statement that is true for you or your child.

❑ 1. I give my child a lot of love and support.

❑ 2. My child can come to me for advice and support. We have frequent, in-depth conversations.

❑ 3. My child knows three or more other adults that he or she can go to for advice and support.

❑ 4. Our neighbors encourage and support my child.

❑ 5. My child's school provides a caring, encouraging environment.

❑ 6. I'm actively involved in helping my child succeed in school.

❑ 7. My child feels valued by adults in our community.

❑ 8. My child is given useful roles in our community.

❑ 9. My child serves in our community one or more hours each week.

❑ 10. My child feels safe at home, at school, and in our neighborhood.

❑ 11. Our family has clear rules and consequences for behavior. We monitor each other's whereabouts.

❑ 12. My child's school has clear rules and consequences for behavior.

❑ 13. Our neighbors take responsibility for monitoring my child's behavior.

❏ 14. I model positive, responsible behavior, and so do other adults that my child knows.

❏ 15. My child's best friends model responsible behavior.

❏ 16. I encourage my child to do well, and so do my child's teachers.

❏ 17. My child spends three or more hours each week in lessons or practice in music, theater, or other arts.

❏ 18. My child spends three or more hours each week in school or community sports, clubs, or organizations.

❏ 19. My child spends one or more hours each week in religious services or participating in spiritual activities.

❏ 20. My child spends two or fewer nights each week out with friends "with nothing special to do."

❏ 21. My child wants to do well in school.

❏ 22. My child likes to learn new things.

❏ 23. My child does an hour or more of homework each school day.

❏ 24. My child cares about her or his school.

❏ 25. My child reads for pleasure three or more hours each week.

❏ 26. My child believes that it's really important to help other people.

❏ 27. My child wants to help promote equality and reduce world poverty and hunger.

❏ 28. My child acts on his or her convictions. My child stands up for his or her beliefs.

❏ 29. My child tells the truth–even when it's not easy.

❏ 30. My child accepts and takes personal responsibility for her or his actions and decisions.

❏ 31. My child believes that it's important not to be sexually active or to use alcohol or other drugs.

❏ 32. My child is good at planning ahead and making decisions.

❏ 33. My child is good at making and keeping friends.

❏ 34. My child knows and is comfortable with people of different cultural, racial, and/or ethnic backgrounds.

❏ 35. My child resists negative peer pressure and avoids dangerous situations.

❏ 36. My child tries to resolve conflicts nonviolently.

❏ 37. My child believes that he or she has control over many things that happen to him or her.

❏ 38. My child feels good about herself or himself.

❏ 39. My child believes that his or her life has a purpose.

❏ 40. My child is optimistic about her or his future.

Building External Assets

Support

Young people need to experience support, care, and love from their families and many others. They need organizations and institutions that provide positive, supportive environments.

The more love, support, and adult contacts a young person has, the more likely it is that he or she will grow up healthy.

The support assets are:

1. Family support
2. Positive family communication
3. Other adult relationships
4. Caring neighborhood
5. Caring school climate
6. Parent involvement in schooling.

ASSET #1
Family Support

Kids feel loved and supported in their family.

> **64%** *of the youth we surveyed have this asset in their lives.*

At Home

▶ Give more hugs and verbal reinforcement. Don't assume that your kids know how much you love them. Tell them.

▶ Let your love for your children show in the way you look at them, the words you say, your tone of voice, and your body language.

▶ It's not true that all kids want their parents to stop hugging or kissing them once they become teenagers. Ask your children to tell you what feels comfortable for them, and respect their boundaries.

▶ Eat at least one meal together every day.

▶ Set aside at least one evening per week for family activities. Brainstorm as a family things you might like to do, then agree on which ones to try. Be open to ideas from all family members, and be willing to share your children's interests.

▶ Spend time with each of your children individually. Try to make this a daily event—ten minutes after school, a half-hour in the evening, an hour on Saturday morning. Let them know that your time together is important to you, too.

- ▶ Talk with your kids about what would make your home more comfortable and inviting for them and their friends. Take steps to address any concerns.
- ▶ Be loving toward yourself and your spouse or partner. Children learn to love by example.
- ▶ Be your children's biggest fan.

At School

- ▶ Educate parents on how to be supportive of their children. Check with your school counselor or social worker for suggestions.
- ▶ Regularly call or write parents to give positive messages about their child's attitude or progress, or to report on something the child did that deserves praise and recognition. Do this as often as you can—once every month, three or four times during the school year, or whatever is possible for you.
- ▶ During school conferences and parent meetings, focus on the positive.

In the Community

- ▶ Offer workshops for parents on positive parenting skills. Invite experts to speak on ways for parents to show love and support to their children. Allow time for parents to share their ideas and experiences.
- ▶ Provide and publicize family crisis hotlines. These give family members a chance to "cool off" during a conflict. Train hotline counselors to suggest appropriate ways to respond to conflict, and to refer parents to other resources.

▶ When children call their parents–at the office, the community center, the club, or wherever–make it a priority that parents receive the call.

In the Congregation

▶ Sponsor family nights as a regular part of your youth programming.

▶ Sponsor celebrations of children and families.

▶ Regularly offer parent education as part of the congregation's educational programs.

▶ Make sure that your youth program isn't over-planned. Leave time for families to spend together.

ASSET #2

Positive Family Communication

Kids turn to their parents for advice and support. They have frequent, in-depth conversations with each other on a variety of topics. Parents are approachable and available when kids want to talk.

26% *of the youth we surveyed have this asset in their lives.*

At Home

▶ Be available whenever and wherever your kids want to talk. What if you're in the middle of something? Arrange a time when you can talk–soon. *Tip:* Watch for hints. A child who hangs around usually wants to talk.

▶ When your kids talk, really *listen.* Accept the fact that you won't agree on everything. Never label a child's opinions, beliefs, feelings, or experiences "silly," "stupid," "childish," or "wrong."

▶ Ask your kids *every day* about what they are doing and thinking. Tell them about your day, too. Form the habit of frequent conversation.

▶ Have family dinners now and then during which conversation focuses on one topic. Brainstorm as a family things you might talk about, then rotate whose turn it is to pick the topic.

▶ Spend one hour a week with each child individually. Whenever possible, spend a whole day together. Your kids will cherish these special times.

▶ The fewer topics you declare "off limits," the more your kids will talk to you. If you don't know the answer to a question, help your kids to find it. Visit the library, ask an expert, or search the Internet together.

▶ Be willing to talk in a place that's comfortable for your child. And remember that some kids have a hard time sitting still. Don't insist that they "settle down" before you can talk.

▶ Ask your child's opinion or advice about something important.

At School

▶ Include conversations with parents as part of home- work assignments. *Example:* If you're teaching about the 1980s, you might assign parent interviews— "Where were you in 1985, and what were you doing?"

▶ Provide parents with information about how to respond to tough questions and address sensitive issues. Check with your school counselor or social worker about handouts and brochures on alcohol and other drugs, HIV/AIDS, teen pregnancy, sexual behavior, and other difficult topics. Many parents want to talk with their kids about these subjects, but they don't know where to start or what to say.

▶ Interact with students so they learn to interact with others.

▶ Help students develop a feelings vocabulary—a variety of words they can use to express a variety of feelings. Use posters, films, and literature to explore feelings and ways to express them.

In the Community

▶ Sponsor discussion nights for parents and teens. Publicize the topics in advance.

▶ Teach parents how to respond appropriately when kids want to talk about difficult issues. Offer workshops and community meetings on topics of concern to your community. Invite experts to speak on ways to communicate with kids of all ages.

▶ Sponsor activities and events that bring young people and parents together. Build in time for conversation.

In the Congregation

▶ Plan parent-teen events that encourage conversation—dinners, retreats, discussion groups.

▶ Provide families with conversation-starter questions in the worship bulletin. Sponsor discussion groups for parents and teens.

▶ Teach communication skills to young people and adults. Include ideas and suggestions in mailings to member households.

▶ Let parents know that there is someone on staff who is available to answer their questions, offer advice, or just listen. Kids aren't the only ones who need someone to talk to.

ASSET #3
Other Adult Relationships

Kids know other adults besides their parents they can turn to for advice and support. They have frequent, in-depth conversations with them. Ideally, three or more adults play this role in their lives.

> **41%** *of the youth we surveyed have this asset in their lives.*

At Home

▶ Give your children opportunities to spend time with other adults—trusted neighbors, favorite teachers, or relatives they feel comfortable with and like being around.

▶ Encourage your children to join adult-sponsored groups, troops, or teams.

▶ If your children have special interests, hobbies, or passions, arrange for them to meet adult friends of yours who share their interests.

▶ Take family vacations with other families.

▶ When you invite friends over for social occasions, include your children and theirs in your plans and your conversations.

▶ Get involved in your neighborhood and community. Introduce your children to people you meet.

- Many schools, youth organizations, and congregations have people on staff—guidance counselors, psychologists, and others—who are specially trained to work with young people. Encourage your children to meet them and talk with them.

- With your child, identify the adults who regularly interact with him or her. *Examples:* teachers, coaches, club leaders, bus drivers, employers, administrators, custodians, neighbors, other family members, the parents of their friends. Write a brief note to each one, expressing your appreciation for their care, dedication, and interest in your child.

- Get to know your children's friends. Welcome them into your home.

At School

- Have an open-door policy for students who want to talk. Be available as often as you can before and after school.

- Take time to ask students at least one question about themselves at every student conference or one-on-one meeting.

- Don't consider it wasted time when teachers spend time talking with students.

- Occasionally eat lunch in the cafeteria with the students.

- Be the faculty sponsor for a student club or event.

- Let parents know that there are people on staff who are willing and available to talk with kids.

- Work with people in your community to arrange mentoring, internship, and service-learning opportunities for students.

In the Community

▶ Build at least one sustained, caring relationship with a child or adolescent, either informally or through a community program. Talk with kids who live near you or work with you.

▶ Teach coaches and other adult leaders how to communicate well with teens. Encourage them to get to know the young people they interact with.

▶ Create opportunities for youth and adults to work and play together.

▶ Offer mentoring programs that match kids with caring adults. Volunteer to be a mentor.

▶ Sponsor career days so young people can spend time with adults in professions that interest them.

▶ Pair kids with adult volunteers for community service projects.

In the Congregation

▶ Train adult volunteers to talk with kids who have concerns. Publicize the fact that these volunteers are available and accessible.

▶ Sponsor a congregational mentoring program.

▶ Plan intergenerational programs and events so kids and adults can get to know each other.

ASSET #4
Caring Neighborhood

Kids feel that their neighbors support them, encourage them, and care about them.

> **40%** *of the youth we surveyed have this asset in their lives.*

At Home

▶ Introduce your children to your neighbors. If you don't know your neighbors, introduce yourself.

▶ Revive the old tradition of welcoming new neighbors with a plate of cookies or a cake.

▶ Get to know your neighbors. *Examples:* Work together on a neighborhood block party or cleanup; organize a potluck picnic or cookout; plan activities to bring adults and kids together; join or start a neighborhood group or watch club.

▶ Learn the names of every young person in your neighborhood. Smile at them and greet them by name when you see them.

▶ Show interest in your neighbors' children. When you see your neighbors, ask about their kids. Say something positive about them.

▶ Get to know five kids in your neighborhood.

▶ Recruit volunteers (senior citizens, college students, or stay-at-home parents) to wait with children at school bus stops.

▶ Encourage your children to find ways to serve in your neighborhood.

At School

▶ Invite students to identify ways they can promote caring in their neighborhoods.

▶ Assign projects that promote interaction between students and their neighbors. *Example:* Have students interview a neighbor, then report back on what they learned about her or him.

▶ Encourage students to find ways to serve in their neighborhoods. Brainstorm ideas together.

▶ Whether your school is a "neighborhood school" (drawing most of its students from the immediate area) or not, be neighborly. *Examples:* Hold an open house for people in your neighborhood; form alliances with neighborhood groups and businesses; make your auditorium available for neighborhood meetings; schedule times when your gym may be used by youth and adults from the neighborhood. If you have a computer lab, offer free or inexpensive classes for neighbors, with free public access to the Internet.

▶ Provide opportunities for youth to serve the school neighborhood. Contact a neighborhood group to learn about activities it has planned for the future, and ask if your students can help.

▶ Encourage adults in your neighborhood to volunteer in your school. *Example:* Have seniors visit as lunchtime listeners, sitting at the cafeteria tables and talking with students.

In the Community

▶ Encourage your friends and neighbors to get to know the young people who live around them and to make youth a priority.

▶ Sponsor neighborhood get-togethers. *Examples:* block parties, potluck dinners, ice-cream socials, fall festivals, carnivals.

▶ Organize informal activities (such as pick-up basketball) for neighborhood youth.

▶ Let kids in your neighborhood know that your house is a "safe house"—someplace they can go for help or extra support.

▶ Work with children and teenagers to create a neighborhood garden, playground, or park.

▶ Start a neighborhood newsletter or newspaper; create a neighborhood Web page; publish a neighborhood directory.

▶ Support neighborhood groups. Work to strengthen neighborhood watch programs.

▶ Gather representatives from several neighborhoods and develop plans and strategies for creating caring neighborhoods. Involve kids.

In the Congregation

▶ Encourage all members to get to know young people in their neighborhoods. Emphasize the importance of caring neighborhoods for youth, and provide ideas for action.

▶ Encourage children and teens to form relationships with their neighbors. *Examples:* Schedule potluck dinners, ice-cream socials, and other get-togethers to which youth may invite a neighbor.

▶ Be a positive presence in your neighborhood. *Examples:* Sponsor a neighborhood social for adults and youth; start a drop-in day-care center; start an after-school program; provide opportunities for youth to serve the neighborhood.

ASSET #5
Caring School Climate

Kids feel that their school supports them, encourages them, and cares about them.

> **24%** *of the youth we surveyed have this asset in their lives.*

At Home

▶ Ask your children how they feel about school. Do they perceive it as a caring, nurturing place? Why or why not? Encourage them to give specific reasons for the way they feel.

▶ Have your child name people at school who show that they care about students. Write a personal note of thanks and appreciation to everyone your child names.

▶ Get involved with a parent-teacher organization. Work to create a spirit of cooperation.

▶ Invite your child's teacher(s) to dinner at your home.

▶ Volunteer at your child's school. *Examples:* Help out in the classroom; tutor kids in reading or math; spend time in the library or media center; chaperon field trips and school events.

▶ Thank your children's teachers for the good work they do.

At School

▶ Learn the names of as many students as you can. Smile at them and greet them by name when you see them.

▶ Start a lunchtime, study hall, or after-school discussion group for students who want to "just talk."

▶ Get to know your students on a personal level. Ask them about their interests, hobbies, passions, goals, hopes, and dreams.

▶ Nurture a sense of school ownership in students by involving them in decision making. *Examples:* Have students create their own list of class or school rules; invite their input on ways to improve the cafeteria, gym, school grounds, or media center; form student committees to address specific problems.

▶ Create an environment where everyone—students, teachers, administrators, staff, visitors, parents, and other volunteers—feels welcome.

▶ Plan extracurricular activities that bring students, teachers, administrators, and staff together for fun and fellowship.

▶ Conduct a schoolwide survey to learn students' opinions about the school climate. Work with youth to frame the questions and the look of the survey. Questions might include "What do you like best about our school?" "What do you like least about our school?" "What would you change to make our school more caring?" Tabulate and publicize the results. Form student-teacher-staff committees to address areas of concern and implement ideas gathered from the surveys.

In the Community

▶ Support your local schools. Acknowledge and honor those that are known for their caring climates. Vote yes for referendums that lower class sizes and improve facilities.

▶ Feature caring schools, teachers, and administrators in newspaper articles and local television programs.

▶ Hold community forums on the topic of caring schools. Invite school administrators to attend. Ask residents for recommendations on how local schools can support and nurture students.

▶ Encourage all adults to volunteer in the schools, not just parents of students.

In the Congregation

▶ Hold roundtable discussions on the topic of caring schools. Invite parents and kids to share their ideas and concerns. Summarize them and communicate them to area schools.

▶ Identify the teachers, school administrators, and other educators among your membership. Acknowledge and honor their efforts.

▶ Encourage members to volunteer in schools.

▶ When the youth group looks for service projects, don't forget nearby schools. *Examples:* Young people might volunteer to paint, work on the grounds, make repairs, or help out in other ways.

ASSET #6

Parent Involvement in Schooling

Parents are actively involved in helping young people succeed in school. They talk with their kids about school, sometimes assist with schoolwork, and attend school events.

> **29%** *of the youth we surveyed have this asset in their lives.*

At Home

▶ Speak with each of your child's teachers in person at least once during the school year. Call to check in every other month.

▶ Regularly ask your kids what they are learning in school. Offer to help with homework in appropriate ways. *Example:* It's okay to help a child plan a special paper, and to be available for advice, suggestions, or rides to the library. It's *not* okay to write the paper.

▶ When you receive a school calendar, enter important dates and events onto your family calendar. Make attending school events a family priority.

▶ Join the parent-teacher organization at your child's school. If you can't volunteer a lot of time, say so.

▶ Volunteer to do what you can to help out at your child's school. *Examples:* Be a room parent, chaperon school functions, serve on committees.

▶ If you're concerned about circumstances or events at your child's school, talk to teachers and administrators. If you feel that you're not being heard, talk to other parents about constructive ways to address your concerns.

▶ In general, parents tend to be *most* involved with their children's education during elementary school, *less* involved during middle and high school. Make it a point to stay actively involved for as long as your child is in school.

At School

▶ Personally contact each student's family at least once during the school year.

▶ Form a parent advisory committee to give input into school policy decisions.

▶ Send notes home to parents frequently about what students are working on and learning in class.

▶ If you publish a class newsletter, print additional copies for your students to bring home to their parents.

In the Community

▶ Coordinate activities with the school(s) so parents and kids don't have to choose between school events and community events.

▶ On days when schools have open houses and parent-teacher conferences, provide activities for younger children so parents are free to participate without child-care concerns.

▶ Allow and encourage employees to volunteer time at schools.

In the Congregation

▶ Don't schedule activities for youth that conflict with important school activities.

▶ Encourage parents to show an interest in their children's school experience and to take any concerns they have to the school.

▶ Offer workshops for parents on how to get involved and stay involved in their children's schools.

Tips for Teens: Build Your Own Assets

Asset #1: Family Support

GOAL: A family that is loving and supportive, and a home that is a comfortable place to be.

If you want your home to be warm, caring, comfortable, supportive, and fun, do your part to make it that way. Replace put-downs with affirmations, teasing with supporting, thinking "me" with thinking "we." Show some affection, show some interest, and listen when other people want to talk. Treat the people in your family the way you want them to treat you. These ideas may sound simple, but they can make a big difference.

Asset #2: Positive Family Communication

GOAL: Parents you can turn to for advice, support, and in-depth conversations about serious issues.

When you ask your parents for advice or support, do you get a lecture? For most parents, giving advice is an almost irresistible urge. You might try explaining that sometimes all you really need them to do is listen while you sort things out. Or suggest a compromise: You talk, they listen, and ten minutes later (or an hour, or a day) you listen to what they have to say.

Here's another idea you might want to try: Find things your parents are really good at, then focus on those. *Examples:* If your mom is a math whiz, turn to her when you're worried about the math final. If your dad likes to write, ask for his advice on the article you're writing for your school newspaper.

If you feel that you can't talk to your parents about serious things, maybe it's because they still treat you like a child. Sometimes it's hard for parents to accept that children grow up and form their own beliefs and opinions. If there's another adult in your life you can talk to—someone who values your opinions and treats you with respect—try to arrange a meeting between you, your parents, and the other adult. Maybe your parents will see you through that person's eyes.

It's normal for kids and parents to disagree. Try to stay calm, and keep your voice down. Meanwhile, make an effort to see your parents' point of view. You'll be setting a good example for them to follow.

Asset #3: Other Adult Relationships

GOAL: Three or more adults besides your parents you can turn to for advice, support, and in-depth conversations about serious issues.

If you don't have other adults to talk to, start looking in the places you normally go—your school, place of worship, scout troop, neighborhood park or community center. You'll probably find adults who enjoy spending time with young people. Or see if there's a teen clinic in your area. Most (if not all) offer counseling, not just medical advice.

Join an adult-sponsored group, troop, or team. Meet your neighbors. Talk to your school counselor, have a heart-to-heart with a favorite aunt or uncle, or get to know your friends' parents. Form a relationship with a mentor in your community, congregation, or youth program. You *will* find adults you can talk to, if you're willing to reach out.

Asset #4: Caring Neighborhood

GOAL: Neighbors who support you, encourage you, and care about you.

You can do a lot to create a caring neighborhood. Start by introducing yourself to adults and other youth you see. Say hi to younger kids, too. Be a friend and role model to them.

Get to know your neighbors. Smile at them and greet them when you see them on the street, and spend a few moments talking with them. If you notice that they need assistance—carrying groceries, opening a door, hauling a stroller up the stairs—offer to help. Ask a neighbor to teach you something, such as how to bake bread or change a tire. Find out about neighborhood events (block parties, socials) and get involved.

It's likely that many people in your neighborhood don't know the children and teenagers who live there. You can help your neighborhood become more child-friendly by creating a newsletter that gives information about the events and people in your neighborhood. Ask younger kids to help you gather the information; ask other teenagers to help produce the newsletter on a computer; ask kids to help distribute the newsletter to every home. Make sure that *you* know the names of everyone on your block or in your building.

Be aware that some adults are intimidated by groups of kids, especially teenagers. If you and several friends are walking down the street and you see a neighbor you know, stop and say hello. If you're walking toward each other, don't make your neighbor walk around you. Move out of the way so he or she can pass.

Asset #5: Caring School Climate

GOAL: A school where you feel cared about, encouraged, and supported.

When you're involved in school activities, you're more likely to feel cared about and supported than if you're on the outside looking in. Try out for a team, run for student council, write for the school paper, join (or start) a service group. If you're not sure what opportunities exist in your school, ask a teacher or administrator.

Do your part to treat other students well and help them to feel cared about and supported. Reach out to kids who seem isolated or lonely and aren't included in cliques or groups. When you're choosing teams for gym class activities or after-school sports, don't just choose your friends. Make it clear that you won't tolerate bullying, and stick up for kids who are bullied by others. Respect school property and encourage other students to do the same.

Encourage your parents to volunteer in your school. Schools become stronger and more caring when parents are active and informed.

Asset #6: Parent Involvement in Schooling

GOAL: Parents who are actively involved in helping you succeed in school.

Talk to your parents about school. Tell them about your day, your successes, your frustrations. Share funny stories with them. Ask them to help you with a school project or a tricky homework problem.

If your teachers send notes, schedules, and announcements home with you, be sure to give them to your parents. Offer to write important school events on the family calendar. Remind your parents of special events a few days in advance. Let them know that you really *want* them to be involved.

Empowerment

Young people need to be valued by their community and have opportunities to contribute to others. For this to occur, they must be safe and feel secure.

The more a young person is valued and feels valuable, the more likely it is that she or he will grow up healthy.

The empowerment assets are:

7. Community values youth
8. Youth as resources
9. Service to others
10. Safety.

ASSET #7

Community Values Youth

Kids perceive that adults in the community value young people.

> **20%** *of the youth we surveyed have this asset in their lives.*

At Home

▶ Ask your kids what makes them feel valued. *Tips:* Children and youth feel valued when 1) adults take time to be with them; 2) adults listen to them and take seriously what they have to say; and 3) adults seek them out and solicit their feedback.

▶ Point out to your children how your town or city currently uses resources to help kids prosper. *Examples:* parks, recreation programs, youth programs. Ask if they have ideas about how your town or city can do more.

▶ Talk with your children about where they feel valued in the community and where they don't. Encourage them to spend most of their time in places where they feel valued.

▶ Have regular family meetings to plan, solve problems, and encourage each other. Rotate who leads the meetings.

▶ Role-play positive and appropriate ways for kids to respond when community members treat them disrespectfully.

▶ Attend community events as a family. You'll improve your child's perceptions of your community–and vice versa.

▶ Affirm and support your children's friends. Let them know that you value them.

At School

▶ Ask students to create pictures or stories of what a community looks and feels like when it values youth. Disseminate these pictures and stories widely.

▶ Form partnerships with community organizations through which students can volunteer and/or develop mentoring relationships with adults.

▶ Invite community members to a school open house hosted by students. Invite neighbors to functions that showcase students' work and creativity. *Examples:* school plays, science fairs, athletic events.

▶ Regularly invite people from the community to speak to students about their careers, volunteer activities, or other areas of interest.

▶ Encourage students to get involved in community service.

▶ Create leadership roles for youth. Are there students on your school board? Do students sit on decision-making committees?

In the Community

▶ Instead of viewing kids as problems, start viewing them as assets.

▶ Use focus groups to find out 1) how kids think the community perceives them and 2) how they feel they are treated by adults in the community. Identify and target problem areas and celebrate successes.

▶ Educate adults in ways to show kids they matter. (See the tips in the first bullet under "At Home," page 56.)

▶ Allow and encourage youth involvement in neighborhood and community organizations.

▶ Give positive feedback to youth you encounter in stores (as clerks, sales help, wait staff, etc.) when you notice them doing a good job.

▶ Publicize and celebrate the ways young people contribute to the community.

▶ Challenge negative stereotypes of youth in the media.

▶ Display youth artwork and projects at local stores, community centers, and other places where community members are likely to see them.

▶ Thank people who work with children and youth (teachers, youth group leaders, social service providers, clergy, etc.). Show that you value them, too.

In the Congregation

▶ Welcome youth as part of the congregation, rather than as a separate group. Give them meaningful roles—as greeters, ushers, teachers for younger kids—and recognize them for their contributions.

▶ Include youth in leadership so they are valued by the members of the congregation.

▶ Maintain year-round connections with youth. Don't lose contact over the summer.

▶ Form a youth issues committee made up of youth.

▶ Educate members about negative stereotypes of youth and ways to overcome them.

ASSET #8

Youth as Resources

Kids are given useful roles in the community.

> **24%** *of the youth we surveyed have this asset in their lives.*

At Home

▶ Involve your children in family decisions. Ask for their input and advice. Take their interests, talents, and opinions seriously.

▶ Have a family meeting and get everyone's ideas on accomplishing household tasks. Share the decisions and share the work.

▶ Ask your children to help you plan family reunions, family outings, or neighborhood gatherings.

▶ Provide your children with age-appropriate roles that contribute to your family's well-being. *Examples:* planning and preparing meals, doing meaningful chores, helping younger siblings with homework, helping adults with significant tasks. Remind them often that their roles are important to the family as a whole.

▶ Instead of buying gifts for birthdays and holidays, commission your children to make some of the gifts.

▶ Use some of your home projects as teaching opportunities. *Examples:* With your child, build a birdhouse, fix a bike, paint a room, or plant a garden.

▶ Ask your child to teach you something—current slang, a hobby, a song, a skill, how to navigate the Internet.

▶ Encourage your children to share their talents and gifts with others.

At School

▶ Include students in school decision making. *Examples:* Students might sit on planning committees, produce the school handbook, or prepare the agenda for the annual open house.

▶ Teach youth how to positively exert their influence in community affairs. *Examples:* Teach them specific social action skills including telephoning, surveying, polling, and speechmaking.

▶ Give student councils real authority over some issues.

▶ Engage young people as active planners in some aspects of their education. *Examples:* Let them choose independent study projects or report topics.

▶ Have students work together to develop a proposal for an extracurricular activity they would like to see available in their school.

▶ Empower kids and teens by teaching them how to teach others. *Examples:* Older students might tutor, read to, or develop mentor relationships with younger students. Peers might teach peers. Offer extra credit to youth who teach or help other students.

▶ Cultivate leadership skills in many students, not just a select few.

In the Community

▶ Work to encourage the perception that youth are *resources* with skills, talents, and abilities to be tapped, as opposed to *problems* to be controlled.

▶ Train community agencies, neighborhood groups, and programs in ways to increase youth involvement in decision making.

▶ Include young people on neighborhood and community boards and councils. Give them opportunities to take leadership roles and make real contributions.

▶ Get youth involved in your organization or business.

▶ Publicize volunteer programs and opportunities for young people.

▶ Create win-win situations. Make sure that all sides at all levels see the benefits of working together.

▶ Hire youth when appropriate. *Example:* You might hire students to serve as election judges, or to create and update city and community Web pages.

In the Congregation

▶ Ask for youth input in congregational decisions.

▶ Provide many opportunities for youth to be leaders in and contributors to the congregation. Regularly include them as leaders of worship services and other intergenerational events.

▶ Revise your planning process as needed to include youth as vision bearers, idea makers, speakers, etc.

▶ Involve youth in caring for and teaching younger children.

▶ Include youth on volunteer committees.

ASSET #9
Service to Others

Kids serve in the community
one or more hour per week.

50% *of the youth we surveyed
have this asset in their lives.*

At Home

▶ Be a role model for your children by serving others.

▶ Set aside two hours one weekend for serving others
as a family. *Examples:* Pick up litter in a park; volunteer at a soup kitchen or shelter.

▶ Brainstorm ten or more ways your family can serve
others. Vote on one to do, pick a date, and do it.
Afterward, talk about your experience. *Tip:* You don't
need to commit to a large project. Service can be as
simple as visiting someone who's homebound or bak-
ing cookies for the family across the hall.

▶ Together with your child, help a neighbor. *Examples:*
Shovel snow for an elderly person; take a child to the
library or playground.

▶ Talk with your children about the benefits of serving
others. These include 1) personal satisfaction, 2) learning to get along better with others, 3) acquiring new
skills, 4) coming into contact with many different kinds
of people, 5) learning patience, and 6) making a difference in the world.

▶ Encourage your kids to participate in service activities through their school, youth organization, or congregation.

At School

▶ Include service learning as part of the regular school curriculum.

▶ Place as much emphasis on celebrating service as on rewarding athletic or academic achievement. *Examples:* Hold awards ceremonies for students who serve; publish articles about them in the school newspaper; give "service letters" and scholarships.

▶ Train teenagers how to help, tutor, and befriend younger children.

▶ Invite local residents to serve your school. *Examples:* Neighbors might tutor students, mentor them, read to them, or sit with them at lunchtime.

▶ Encourage student groups to serve the school neighborhood.

▶ Have students collect items for distribution to needy families in your neighborhood or community.

In the Community

▶ Create and publicize service opportunities for youth and families.

▶ Ask kids how they would like to serve. Match opportunities to their interests and abilities.

▶ Teach neighborhoods, congregations, and civic organizations how to involve youth in service efforts.

▶ Make volunteering convenient for children and teens. *Examples:* Schedule service projects for after-school and weekend hours; provide transportation and adult supervision; donate needed supplies, building materials, etc.

▶ Recognize youth who serve. *Examples:* Praise them in community publications; have an annual awards banquet at your community center.

▶ Create neighborhood service projects that bring adults and children together.

In the Congregation

▶ Make service a core value in your congregation. Speak of it often; write about it in publications and newsletters that go out to members; create flags and banners about it; honor members of all ages who serve.

▶ Make service a central component of youth programming.

▶ Create intergenerational service projects—opportunities for adults and kids to work together. Include youth in congregation-wide service projects.

▶ Form a partnership with a community agency that needs regular help and/or financial assistance. Engage members of all generations in that partnership.

▶ Address social issues in youth education, and provide opportunities for youth to address those issues through service. *Examples:* hunger, illiteracy, homelessness.

ASSET #10
Safety

Kids feel safe at home, at school, and in their neighborhood

55% *of the youth we surveyed have this asset in their lives.*

At Home

▶ Don't tolerate hurtful words or actions in your home. Model loving, respectful behavior toward your spouse, children, other family members, and friends.

▶ Set clear family ground rules about maintaining physical and emotional safety within the family. Talk about things that make people feel safe and unsafe. Seek professional help if any family member violates the physical or emotional safety of another.

▶ Establish simple but firm house rules about answering the telephone, opening the door to strangers, spending time at home alone, using appliances, watching TV, surfing the Internet, and respecting curfews.

▶ Keep track of all family members' whereabouts and plans. Let each other know about changes.

▶ Together with your children, meet and get to know as many people in your neighborhood as possible. Watch out for their safety and ask them to do the same for you.

▶ Work with your neighbors to address safety needs and concerns in the neighborhood.

▶ Talk with your children about what to do if they feel unsafe at school, on the street, in the park, or anywhere they go. Make sure they understand that they can tell you about bad things that happen to them.

▶ Walk or drive your child's friends home after dark, even if they live nearby.

At School

▶ Make it a priority to create a safe environment in the school building, on school grounds, and at school activities. Ask kids what makes them feel unsafe at school, solicit their input on ways to make school safer, and act on their suggestions.

▶ Actively work to create an environment that accepts, welcomes, and celebrates diversity. Don't tolerate bullying or disrespect of any kind.

▶ Keep student-teacher ratios low so teachers can spend more time teaching and less time trying to manage students' behavior.

▶ Set and enforce a no-tolerance policy regarding weapons, violence, harassment, and racial incidents. Establish an anonymous way for students to report when others violate these boundaries.

▶ Teach children how to tell adults about bad things that happen to them.

▶ Establish a peer mediation program so students can help each other resolve conflicts peacefully.

▶ Encourage teachers, administrators, and staff members to get to know students and watch out for their safety.

▶ Provide information and training to students about how to protect their safety and the safety of others.

In the Community

▶ Meet with teenagers in your community to find out where they do and don't feel safe. Ask what could be done to help them feel safer.

▶ Provide young people with safe, supervised times and places where they can hang out with their friends.

▶ Make safety a high priority in parks and other public places.

▶ Coordinate residents to provide safe places where young people can go if they feel threatened. *Example:* Have at least one McGruff House on every block.

▶ Promote and support neighborhood watch programs, block clubs, DARE (Drug Abuse Resistance Education), Safety Camp, National Night Out, and other crime-prevention, community-building efforts.

▶ Make sure that youth have access to services (hotlines, counselors, etc.) for times when their safety is violated.

In the Congregation

▶ Create a safe environment for youth in the congregation. Monitor adults who work with youth, and avoid situations where safety could be compromised.

▶ Make your building a safe haven for kids in trouble.

▶ Educate the entire congregation on how members can help youth feel safe at home, at school, and in their community.

▶ Work for community change that can make neighborhoods safer for children and teens.

Tips for Teens: Build Your Own Assets

Asset #7: Community Values Youth

GOAL: A community where you feel and perceive that you and other young people are appreciated and valued.

Think about your experiences as a community member. Do you feel valued? Dismissed? Appreciated? Scorned? Why do you feel as you do? Are there people in your community who make you feel worthwhile—and others who make you feel worthless? What can you do to improve the way youth are perceived and treated in your community?

You might show that you value your community by getting involved in a neighborhood project. Question adults when they negatively stereotype youth, and offer examples of children and teens who are actively working to make the community a better place. Don't be too shy to speak proudly about the ways you're contributing to your community . . . or if you really don't want to talk about yourself, then speak proudly about your friends.

Sometimes we don't realize how much other people value us. You might want to identify four adults you know (a parent, another adult relative, a neighbor, teacher, coach, etc.) and ask each one what he or she thinks of you. Do they see you as an important member of the community? If so, why? Their answers may surprise you.

Asset #8: Youth as Resources

GOAL: A community where you and other young people have useful roles and meaningful things to do.

Look around your community and learn about the many opportunities available to give something back. Where can you contribute? Where can you lead? Can you be an officer in a school club or youth organization? Can you run for student council? Are there neighborhood, town, or city councils or committees that welcome youth involvement? (If they don't welcome it yet, they might with a little encouragement.)

Don't wait to be "given" a useful role. Create one for yourself. Stand up, speak out, and stay informed. Write letters to the editor of your local newspaper on issues that concern you. Lobby for (or against) ordinances or laws. Give a speech on a topic you care about–children's rights, homelessness, domestic violence, education, senior citizens, health care. Develop a skill you can share and teach others. Become an expert on a topic that's important to you–computers, cats, clean water, recycling–and educate others. Campaign for someone who's running for office in your school, city, or state. It's your community, too, and you have the right to be an active, important part of it.

Get other kids involved in your efforts and offer them useful roles. If you're campaigning for a candidate, they can help you hand out flyers. Younger kids love it when older, wiser kids take them seriously and make them feel wanted and needed.

Asset #9: Service to Others

GOAL: To serve in your community one or more hours per week.

Serving in your community is a great way to meet people and find new meaning in life. There are countless ways to serve. Think about your friends, people in your neighborhood, homeless people, elderly people, animals, the environment, your school, your congregation, your youth organization . . . what else? Figure out where you want to serve, then find out what's needed and how you can do the most good. One hour per week is almost no time at all; you probably spend at least that long channel surfing or just hanging out.

If you want to find out how good it feels to serve but you're not quite ready to commit, try this: Do a "secret service" for someone you know. Take out the trash when it's your brother's turn. Leave a treat in a friend's locker or a potted plant on a neighbor's porch. Or talk to people who are active in community service. Ask them what they give–and what they get in return.

If you're not sure where to start serving, check your phone book to see if any of the organizations listed on page 71 have chapters near you. Many welcome young people and give them opportunities to serve.

- ▶ Boys & Girls Clubs of America
- ▶ Boy Scouts of America
- ▶ Girls, Inc.
- ▶ Girl Scouts of the U.S.A.
- ▶ Habitat for Humanity
- ▶ Kids Against Crime
- ▶ Kids Against Pollution
- ▶ Kids for Saving the Earth
- ▶ National Network of Youth Advisory Boards
- ▶ Students Against Destructive Decisions (formerly Students Against Driving Drunk, better known as SADD)
- ▶ Super Volunteers!
- ▶ United Way
- ▶ Youth Service America

Asset #10: Safety

GOAL: To feel safe at home, at school, and in your neighborhood.

Tell your parents about any fears or concerns you have—about your home, neighborhood, parks, school, or anyplace else you go. Describe any events that made you feel worried or afraid. Ask for help from your parents, teachers, religious leaders, or other adults you know and trust. When you live in fear, you're less likely to take healthy risks, try new things, and make positive contributions. If school feels unsafe to you, you might encourage your parents to volunteer at your school and see for themselves what it's like.

Do your part to make your neighborhood, community, and school safer for everyone. Start or join a group, brainstorm ideas, and volunteer to help put your ideas into action. Or choose an issue that interests you and promote safety. *Examples:* crime prevention, accident prevention, disease prevention, emergency first aid, disaster prevention and preparation. You might educate others about fire prevention, bicycle helmets, or emergency services in your community. Suggest that your school or community hold a safety fair, or ask your mayor to proclaim a Safety Week for your town or city. When you work for safety, everyone benefits—including you.

Boundaries and Expectations

Young people need to know what is expected of them and whether activities and behaviors are "in bounds" or "out of bounds."

The more a child has clear, consistent boundaries and high expectations, the more likely it is that he or she will grow up healthy.

The boundaries and expectations assets are:

11. Family boundaries
12. School boundaries
13. Neighborhood boundaries
14. Adult role models
15. Positive peer influence
16. High expectations.

ASSET #11
Family Boundaries

**Parents set clear rules and consequences
for their kids' behavior. They monitor their
children's whereabouts.**

43% *of the youth we surveyed
have this asset in their lives.*

At Home

▶ Talk with your spouse or partner about boundaries
for your children's behavior, and reach agreement.
Kids need parents to stand together.

▶ Talk with your children about the boundaries. Be positive; say what you *want* them to do, not just what you
don't want them to do. Make boundaries clear and
concise—five words or less, if possible.

▶ Once you've articulated your family boundaries,
expect your children to honor them. Don't *suspect*
them of misbehavior without a reason.

▶ Meet monthly to discuss boundaries. Are they fair?
Do they still fit? Do they reflect your family's values
and principles? Adjust them if you need to. If you
need help, read parenting books and seek advice. Be
willing to learn and change.

▶ Regularly renegotiate family rules with teenagers so
they're developmentally appropriate—but know that
even 18-year-olds still need boundaries.

▶ Focus discipline as a way to teach, not as a form of punishment. Never let discipline become an excuse for venting anger. If you need help, call a local crisis hotline and ask for information on support groups for parents.

▶ Have a family calendar on which all family members (including parents) note where they will be and when.

▶ Learn who your children's friends are, then invite their parents to form a "parent network" with you. Agree that children will not be allowed to hold or attend parties without adult supervision.

▶ Make your home an inviting place for your kids and their friends. When they're home, you know where they are!

At School

▶ Respect and reinforce family values and rules as much as possible.

▶ Talk with parents about their standards for their children's conduct, and share with them your standards for student conduct. Find common ground and support each other's efforts.

▶ Include parents in meetings with students regarding problem behaviors and broken rules.

In the Community

▶ Offer workshops for parents on ways to establish boundaries, address problem behaviors, and enforce consequences. Invite experts to speak and field questions.

▶ Offer support groups so parents can learn from each other about establishing and enforcing appropriate family boundaries.

▶ As you set standards for young people's participation in community activities, invite parents to contribute their ideas and suggestions.

▶ Create tip sheets for parents on fair and effective discipline strategies.

▶ Create an agreement form for kids and parents on which they both agree to keep the other informed about their whereabouts. Publicize the form, introduce it at a community meeting, and have copies available.

▶ When you see young people in inappropriate places, take responsibility to ask them whether their parents know where they are.

In the Congregation

▶ Set and enforce clear expectations for the behavior of the youth in your congregation.

▶ Educate parents in how to set appropriate boundaries. Include ideas in worship bulletins and mailings to member households.

▶ Give parents opportunities to talk together about family boundaries.

▶ Educate young people about how to set boundaries for themselves. This would be an excellent topic for a youth retreat.

▶ Provide adequate adult supervision for all youth group events.

ASSET #12
School Boundaries

Schools set clear rules and consequences for student behavior.

46% *of the youth we surveyed have this asset in their lives.*

At Home

▶ Encourage your school to create a conduct code at the beginning of the year, review the code with the students, and send copies home to parents. Suggest that students help to create the code.

▶ Get involved in a parent-teacher policy organization.

▶ Inform yourself about school boundaries by visiting your child's school. Observe how students behave, how adults and students interact with each other, and how conflicts are resolved. If you have questions, take them to your child's teachers or the school principal.

▶ Talk with your child's teachers about boundaries in the classroom. Talk with your child about the importance of respecting those boundaries. If there are some your child doesn't agree with, find out why.

▶ Take time to learn about and discuss school boundaries as a family each school year.

▶ Support school boundaries, consequences, and expectations for students' behavior.

▶ Contact school authorities if you learn that school boundaries are not being enforced fairly, consistently, or appropriately.

▶ When conflicts occur, don't be pushy. Calmly state your concern and suggest solutions.

At School

▶ Create an official school policy on behaviors that are in-bounds (*examples:* learning, caring, respecting differences) and out-of-bounds (*examples:* bullying, violence, cheating, harassment). Establish clear consequences for out-of-bounds behaviors—and ways to affirm in-bounds behaviors. Involve students, parents, and staff in creating this policy. Review it several times a year with everyone in the school community.

▶ If you publish a student handbook, send copies home to parents.

▶ Include youth in establishing boundaries and communicating them to other students.

▶ Expect young people to behave responsibly. When they don't, enforce consequences fairly and consistently.

▶ Post your school boundaries in many places throughout the school—classrooms, halls, cafeteria, auditorium.

▶ Use peer mediation as one way to resolve boundary violations.

▶ Notice and celebrate times when students follow school policies and respect school boundaries.

▶ Provide adequate adult supervision in the lunchroom, in the hallways, on the playground, and other places where students gather.

In the Community

▶ Support school leaders in developing, communicating, and enforcing school boundaries.

▶ As much as possible, make sure that school boundaries are consistent from school to school.

▶ Talk publicly about school boundaries. Let the community know about them so they can support and reinforce them. Post flyers, send mailings, and/or present the boundaries at an open house.

▶ Be sure that coaches and other adult leaders (of teams, clubs, youth organizations, extracurricular activities, after-school programs, etc.) are informed of school boundaries. Ask for their support.

In the Congregation

▶ Learn what the boundaries are in schools in your community. Summarize and publicize them in worship bulletins and mailings to member households. Encourage parents to support them.

▶ Work with schools to define common boundaries that may be taught at school and in the congregation.

▶ Find out about school policies for student behavior. Reinforce those expectations within the congregation.

ASSET #13
Neighborhood Boundaries

Neighbors take responsibility for monitoring young people's behavior.

> **46%** *of the youth we surveyed have this asset in their lives.*

At Home

▶ Hold a front-yard barbecue, block party, or building party to connect with other neighbors. Discuss neighborhood boundaries and identify three or more that everyone can agree on. *Examples:* Respect people and property; report suspicious activity; supervise children younger than 16; end parties by 11:00 P.M.; talk to neighbors directly about concerns. Publish the boundaries in a one-page newsletter and distribute it door-to-door.

▶ As a neighborhood, encourage each other to point out boundaries to youth. *Example:* If a neighbor hears young people swearing, everyone should support the neighbor saying "We don't use that kind of language in our neighborhood."

▶ Notice daily what happens in your neighborhood.

▶ Talk with your children about neighborhood boundaries.

▶ Call other neighbors about concerns or questions. Distribute a neighborhood directory with names, phone numbers, and addresses of neighbors who are interested in participating.

▶ Tell neighbors you trust that you want them to tell you when they see your child behaving inappropriately. Let your child know that you have done this. Encourage neighbors to affirm positive behaviors, too.

▶ Establish and enforce clear boundaries for young people who visit your home.

▶ Welcome new neighbors and introduce them to your neighborhood's boundaries. Invite their suggestions and support.

At School

▶ Talk with students about neighborhood boundaries. Do their neighborhoods have boundaries for young people's behavior? How do they know? Which neighbors seem to notice and care about what they do? How do they (the students) feel about that? Ask students to identify neighbors they perceive as especially caring. They might want to write thank-you notes.

▶ Find out what boundaries exist in the school neighborhood—or set reasonable boundaries and communicate them to students. *Examples:* no littering, no cutting across neighbors' lawns, no loitering on private property, no booming car stereos. Let neighbors know that you have done this.

▶ Survey the school neighborhood to learn if neighbors have any concerns or complaints about student behavior. Communicate these to students and set boundaries to address them.

In the Community

▶ Work to create strong neighborhood bonds. Sponsor activities that encourage neighbors to get to know each other better.

▶ Work with others in the community (individuals, groups, and organizations) to identify and articulate community norms and standards. Include young people in this process.

▶ Work with local businesses, neighborhood organizations, and law enforcement agencies to identify places where kids get into trouble. Start a series of community meetings to brainstorm and implement solutions.

▶ Involve youth in establishing boundaries for public places. *Examples:* parks, playgrounds, shopping malls, community centers. Display flyers or posters listing the boundaries in clear, concise language.

▶ Expect young people to behave responsibly. When they don't, enforce boundaries appropriately.

▶ Enforce curfew laws.

In the Congregation

▶ Set and enforce clear boundaries for youth in the congregation.

▶ When young people behave inappropriately, let them know that you've noticed—and that you expect more of them.

▶ Teach adults in the congregation about the importance of neighborhood boundaries for kids. Encourage them to get to know their neighbors and work with them to establish neighborhood boundaries.

ASSET #14
Adult Role Models

Parents and other adults model positive, responsible behavior.

> **27%** *of the youth we surveyed have this asset in their lives.*

At Home

▶ Always remember that *you* are your child's most important role model. Set high standards for yourself and follow them—even during difficult times. Treat your child with love and respect.

▶ Be involved in your child's life on a daily basis. Spend time together often. Take advantage of "teachable moments"—times and events that invite discussion and learning about positive, responsible behavior.

▶ Talk with your children about adults they know who are positive role models. Find ways to build and strengthen those relationships. Invite friends you respect, admire, and trust to get involved in your children's lives.

▶ Talk with your children about people you see on television, in movies, in magazines and newspapers. Discuss whether they are good role models.

▶ Talk with your children about your own role models. Who do you admire, and why? Who were your role models when you were a child? A teenager? A young adult?

▶ Talk honestly about the issues when you or another adult lets your child down. It's also good role-modeling to apologize for failures and admit mistakes.

At School

▶ Educate *all* staff about the importance of modeling positive, responsible behavior.

▶ Make an extra effort to notice and affirm role models who are of both genders and all ages and races.

▶ Have students identify their heroes. Discuss whether they are good role models. If they are, why? If they aren't, why not?

▶ Focus on positive role models in history, literature, and other subjects.

▶ Expose students to positive adult role models in the community. Invite them into the classroom and school to talk about their lives and interact with students.

▶ Teach students to analyze role models in the media and identify ways they are positive and negative.

In the Community

▶ Volunteer to work with or alongside young people who need positive role models.

▶ Celebrate positive role models in your community through media coverage.

▶ Encourage adults to become mentors for youth.

▶ Honor *all* adults who exhibit the qualities you seek to nurture in youth—not just celebrities or powerful people.

▶ Encourage celebrities and other influential people in your community to model positive, responsible behavior. Remind them that they are role models for youth—real-life heroes.

In the Congregation

▶ Encourage adults to model the kinds of behavior they expect from young people.

▶ Clearly articulate what's expected of *all* people in the congregation.

▶ Provide adult mentors for youth.

▶ Have kids identify role models from your faith tradition. What makes them good role models?

▶ Invite positive role models in the congregation to share their life stories with children and teens.

▶ Encourage adults to get involved with youth groups in your congregation.

▶ Plan intergenerational programs and events so kids can meet adult role models.

ASSET #15
Positive Peer Influence

Children's best friends model responsible
behavior. They are a good influence. They do
well at school and stay away from risky
behaviors such as alcohol and other drug use.

60% *of the youth we surveyed
have this asset in their lives.*

At Home

▶ Invite your children's friends to spend time in your
home. Make them feel welcome and try to get to
know them. Include them in some of your family
activities.

▶ Talk with your kids about their friends. Ask probing
questions. Are they good students? What are their
interests? Do they get along well with their parents?
Try to find out what your children like about their
friends.

▶ Affirm positive friendships without going overboard.
Example: You might say "Jeff seems like a nice kid.
He's funny and easy to be around. I'm glad you invite
him over."

▶ Resist the urge to criticize friendships that seem negative. Many kids get defensive about friends their
parents don't like. This makes them even more determined to maintain the friendships.

▶ Don't jump to conclusions based on what your child's friends look like.

▶ Get to know the parents of your children's friends. Have your kids introduce you at school open houses, community meetings, or activities at your place of worship.

▶ Children learn by example. Ask yourself: Do *your* friends model responsible behavior? Are they a good influence on you?

At School

▶ Train students to be peer counselors or peer helpers. Choose kids who can become good role models and who are liked by their peers.

▶ Provide cooperative learning opportunities for students. Let students work together in groups. Make sure that all children benefit from the cooperative learning experience. For example, the bright students shouldn't spend all or most of their time tutoring other students.

▶ Use class time to teach about friendship. Challenge kids to think about their own friendships. Are they helpful or hurtful? How do they know? Help children develop the skills they need to make and keep good friends.

In the Community

▶ Provide opportunities for young people to model positive, responsible behavior for each other. *Examples:* Promote youth volunteer activities; encourage youth participation on community and city committees.

Helping others through community service is one way to set a great example.

▶ Affirm and honor the healthy choices that youth make. *Examples:* Invite kids to create posters against drug and alcohol use and/or violence, then sign them and display them in the community. Publish the names of honor students in local newspapers. Encourage the media to profile young people who are making a difference in the community.

▶ Sponsor an awards night for young people in the community who serve as good role models. Adults and kids could nominate deserving youth by secret ballot.

In the Congregation

▶ Start a peer helping program. Train young people to be good listeners and to offer appropriate advice and suggestions. Teach them to know when and how to seek help from adults.

▶ Invite young people to think about ways to positively influence their friends in school and in the community. This would be an excellent topic for a weekend youth retreat.

▶ Affirm and honor the young role models in your congregation.

▶ Make friendship a regular topic of discussion within your youth program. Ask kids about their friends. Ask them to think about how their friendships fit with their values.

▶ Sponsor events for youth that include their friends from outside the congregation.

ASSET #16
High Expectations

**Parents and teachers encourage
kids to do well.**

41% *of the youth we surveyed
have this asset in their lives.*

At Home

▶ Expect the best from your kids—each according to his
or her unique abilities. Educate yourself on child
development so you know what's realistic. When
expectations are high yet still within reach, children
will stretch to achieve them.

▶ Periodically check out the expectations you have of
your children, and modify them when necessary.

▶ Notice when your children do well. Let them know
that you admire their talents, abilities, manners,
friendship skills, intelligence, kindness, or whatever
you happen to observe.

▶ Encourage both girls and boys to be independent.

▶ Hold kids accountable for their actions at the same
time you affirm their abilities.

▶ Be on the lookout for new and creative ways to challenge and stimulate your children—without pushing
too hard.

▶ Ask your children what they expect of themselves.
Listen to what they say.

▶ Find and share inspiring stories about people who overcame obstacles in their lives and accomplished amazing things.

▶ Encourage your children to tackle subjects and hobbies that are difficult for them. Work together.

▶ Allow your children to make mistakes and learn from them.

▶ Model the benefits of high expectations by challenging yourself. Take a class, learn a skill, start a hobby, or stretch yourself in other ways.

At School

▶ Tell students what you expect from them.

▶ Talk with parents about expectations. Tell them what you expect from their children; ask them to share their expectations with you. Support each other.

▶ Hold high expectations for *all* students, not just the stars. (Remember that "high" for one student may be "low" for another.)

▶ Encourage students to take positive risks and act on their dreams and ideas. Teach the difference between positive risks and foolish risks.

▶ Give students the tools they need to develop their talents and abilities.

▶ Give kids opportunities to sink or swim. They'll often rise to the occasion. *Example:* Don't always assume that an adult needs to direct an activity. Invite kids to lead and see what happens.

▶ Design learning opportunities that challenge students with all types of learning styles and abilities.

In the Community

▶ Encourage adult leaders (coaches, choir directors, group leaders, volunteer coordinators, etc.) to hold high expectations for *all* young people they work with, not just the stars.

▶ Challenge local media (TV, radio, newspapers) to spotlight the positive accomplishments of many young people, as opposed to the negative actions of a few.

▶ Regularly recognize children and teens who excel in various areas—academics, sports, performance, service, leadership, creativity, courage, etc.

▶ Reassure young people you come into contact with that they can do great things.

▶ Hold high expectations for youth in the workplace—whether you're an employer or a customer.

▶ Sponsor classes and workshops on child development so parents can learn how to set reasonable expectations.

In the Congregation

▶ Tell youth what you expect of them.

▶ Hold high expectations for *all* youth in your congregation, not just the stars.

▶ Give young people opportunities to try new activities or build new skills. Let them know that you expect them to succeed.

▶ Make religious education challenging and interesting.

▶ Educate parents about how to set realistic yet encouraging expectations for their children.

Tips for Teens: Build Your Own Assets

Asset #11: Family Boundaries

GOAL: Parents who set clear rules and consequences for your behavior and monitor your whereabouts.

Boundaries, rules, expectations . . . who needs them? We all do. Life without them would be chaos. Boundaries guide us in making good decisions and provide a structure for our everyday lives. Try thinking of boundaries as *positives* rather than negatives.

Talk with your parents about your family's boundaries. Do you respect and accept them? Why or why not? Do they seem reasonable to you–or totally unfair? Tell your parents how you feel and why. Listen to their side, too, and be respectful. If you can suggest alternatives or compromises, maybe your parents will try things your way. Meanwhile, if you break a rule, accept the consequences. This will *really* impress your parents.

If your parents drive you crazy with questions about where you're going, who with, what for, and how long, beat them to it. Give them the information they want *before* they ask. *Tip:* Put it in the form of a question.

Instead of "Tam and I are going to the 8:00 movie, then out to eat, and I'll be back by midnight," try "I'd like to go to the 8:00 movie with Tam, then out to eat, and be back by midnight. Okay with you?" Then your parents can graciously give their permission. This way, everyone benefits. They get to feel generous, and you get to go out with your friend.

Asset #12: School Boundaries

GOAL: A school that sets clear rules and consequences for students' behavior.

You have the right to attend a school where boundaries are clear and respected—a school where students are free to learn. If your school doesn't fit this description, do something about it.

Form a committee of other students who feel the way you do. Find an adult sponsor—a teacher, coach, or school counselor—who's willing to work with you. Brainstorm a list of problems at your school. *Examples:* cheating, stealing, fighting, weapons, drugs, sexual harassment, racial discrimination, skipping class, students loitering in the halls, swearing, bullying. Then brainstorm fair and clear boundaries for each area—and consequences for infractions. Refine your lists and summarize your work in a Code of Conduct for your school. Present it to your principal and ask for his or her feedback. Work together on a final version. Make sure it's clear, and keep it as concise as you can—one page if possible. Send copies home to parents and post them throughout your school.

Or, if your school publishes a student handbook, you might start there. Is it too long, boring, or out of date? Does it cover all of the problems you see in your school? Your committee might work to revise the handbook.

Asset #13: Neighborhood Boundaries

GOAL: Neighbors who take responsibility for monitoring your behavior.

Picture a neighborhood where people know each other and care about each other. Now picture a neighborhood where people are strangers. Which seems warmer and friendlier to you? Which seems safer? Where would you rather live?

You can help to create a neighborhood where people watch out for each other–including you. Start by getting to know the people who live near you. Begin with the ones who seem friendly. Say hi and introduce yourself. The next time you see them, try a little conversation. You might ask them how long they've lived in the neighborhood and what they like about it. They might respond by asking you a question or two. Before you know it, you'll be talking together. Tell your parents and suggest that they meet your neighbors, too.

Meanwhile, get together with other kids in your neighborhood. Help to set neighborhood standards for safety, noise, or other issues. Agree to treat adults with respect. And start watching out for younger kids, too.

Asset #14: Adult Role Models

GOAL: Parents and other adults who model positive, responsible behavior.

Who are the adult role models in your life? Think of three people you look up to. Include an adult family member (a parent, adult sibling, aunt, uncle, grandparent, or adult cousin), a non-family member (a teacher, coach, neighbor, family friend, or youth group leader you know), and a national or world figure (a leader, celebrity, author, historical figure, or someone else who's been in the news). Now think of why each person is a role model for you. Why do you admire her or him? What special qualities does each person have? Are these qualities you have—or would like to have someday?

Ask adults you know and respect to describe their role models—people who have inspired them or influenced them in positive ways. You might want to learn more about those people or even meet them, if they live near you.

Choose your role models carefully. It's easy to pick famous people (actors, athletes, musicians, singers) because they seem to be everywhere: on the radio, on TV, in magazines and advertisements. But before you decide to be like them, learn more about them. You might discover that the best role models are real people you know.

Asset #15: Positive Peer Influence

GOAL: Friends who are responsible, who avoid risky behaviors, and who have a positive influence on you.

Think of your three or four best friends—the people you spend the most time with and are most influenced by. Do they build you up or drag you down? Do you support each other in making good choices, even when bad choices are easily available? Only you know the answers to these questions. Forget about what your parents think or other people say. How do *you* feel about the friends you have now? If you're not happy with your answer, there are places you can go to meet new people and eventually make new friends. Ask a trusted adult (parent, teacher, youth group leader) for suggestions.

You can also be a positive influence on your friends. When they start to behave in negative ways or take foolish risks, don't go along. Be a peer helper and work to build assets in your friends and yourself.

Asset #16: High Expectations

GOAL: Parents and teachers who encourage you to do well.

Tell your parents your hopes and dreams; tell your teachers what you'd like to accomplish in their classes. Ask for their support. This encourages them to pay closer attention to your progress—and to set high expectations for you.

There's something about high expectations that bring out the best in all of us. When people we know and care about want us to do well, we try harder. High expectations boost our self-esteem. We feel more capable and willing to take positive risks. We're less afraid to make mistakes.

If you feel that your parents or teachers expect too little of you, talk with an adult you know and trust—a youth leader, neighbor, school counselor, or adult relative. Ask for advice and insights. Maybe that person will offer to tell your parents and teachers what a wonderful person you really are.

You can also set high expectations for yourself. Many people have succeeded in life with little or no encouragement from others—and in spite of terrible odds and discouragement. *Tip:* Start a notebook of upbeat, inspiring quotations or sayings, then refer to it when you're feeling down or doubtful about yourself.

Constructive Use of Time

Young people need constructive, enriching opportunities for growth through creative activities, youth programs, congregational involvement, and quality time at home.

The more time a child spends with caring adults who nurture the child's skills and creativity, the more likely it is that she or he will grow up healthy.

The constructive use of time assets are:

17. Creative activities
18. Youth programs
19. Religious community
20. Time at home.

ASSET #17
Creative Activities

**Kids spend three or more hours
each week in lessons or practice in music,
theater, or other arts.**

19% *of the youth we surveyed
have this asset in their lives.*

At Home

▶ Encourage your kids to get involved with the arts. As much as possible, let them choose what to do–play the piano (or the tuba), act or sing, dance, paint, write, draw, throw pots, or whatever interests them. Provide instruments, materials, and lessons (group lessons are fine). Allow and respect practice time.

▶ Show your support by attending your children's performances.

▶ Don't complain when your teenager plays the drums for hours, emotes at the dining room table, sings in the shower, or splatters paint on the basement floor.

▶ Make the arts a part of everyday life in your home. Explore different types of music; attend plays, musicals, concerts, dance performances, films, and operas as a family; visit art museums and cultural centers. Be sure to let your kids choose some of the activities.

▶ If you played an instrument when you were younger, take a refresher course. Then set a good example and practice often. Or join a choir, try out for a play, pick up a paintbrush, or write a poem. Share your excitement with your children.

▶ Be open to a wide variety of arts-related experiences. Scan the newspapers for notices of free performances. Encourage your children to keep you informed about school plays, band concerts, and art exhibits, and attend them as a family.

At School

▶ Provide free access to instruments, art materials, and lessons for students who can't afford them. If the school can't afford them, solicit donations from parents, the community, and local businesses.

▶ When school budgets are tight, music and the arts are often among the first programs to be cut. Lobby hard to keep them at your school. Generate community support.

▶ Use music as a teaching tool in school curricula to reinforce and extend learning. Play background music during classes. While profiling famous people from history, include important musicians and play examples of their music. While exploring different cultures and languages, make music part of your lessons.

▶ Sponsor performances by local artists. Arrange for master classes, where performers share techniques and expertise with young people.

▶ Have a school talent show.

In the Community

▶ Sponsor youth bands, orchestras, drama clubs, dance troupes, and singing groups. Provide places to practice.

▶ Use local talent (youth orchestras, jazz bands, theater troupes, vocal ensembles, garage bands) at community functions. Invite artistic kids to create the banners, posters, and flyers advertising community events.

▶ Check with the schools to find out what they need for their arts programs. Audio equipment? Used musical instruments? Art supplies? Props for plays? Place articles in local newspapers urging community members to contribute.

▶ Sponsor free community events that expose young people (and their families) to a wide variety of arts performances.

▶ Promote appreciation for diversity by sponsoring world music concerts, ethnic dance performances, multicultural festivals, and other events.

In the Congregation

▶ Have a youth band, choir, chorus, or other music group. Or include young people in adult groups.

▶ Especially during the summer months, when it's difficult to gather your complete choir, invite kids to perform solos, duets, or small ensemble pieces.

▶ Be open to featuring a variety of performances in your worship service—from music to skits, dances to poetry readings. Or schedule an all-arts service for one day or evening each month.

▶ Encourage adults in the congregation to offer free lessons to young people as a ministry.

ASSET #18
Youth Programs

Kids spend three or more hours each week in sports, clubs, or organizations at school and/or in the community.

59% *of the youth we surveyed have this asset in their lives.*

At Home

▶ Talk with your children about their interests. Help them to find teams, clubs, or organizations that match or complement their interests. Encourage them to join one—and ask for a six-month commitment. Some kids drop out of programs prematurely, or they skip from one to another without giving any a chance.

▶ Become an adult leader at your child's school. Offer to sponsor or advise an existing school club. Or offer to sponsor a new club in an area that interests you. *Examples:* an amateur astronomers' club, photographers' club, writers' club, cooking club. If you can't volunteer your time, contribute what you can in terms of money or materials.

▶ Start or join a car pool for kids who participate in extracurricular activities.

▶ Set a good example by getting involved with a team, club, or organization that interests you.

At School

▶ Offer extracurricular activities that appeal to a wide variety of needs and interests.

▶ Create a clearinghouse of community youth activities. Post information about community activities on bulletin boards along with school activities. Call attention to them in your daily announcements.

▶ Encourage students to get involved in activities outside of school. When possible, combine or coordinate with school and community organizations and clubs.

▶ Include descriptions of teams, clubs, organizations, and other after-school activities in your student handbook. If your school has a Web site, list them there. Send handouts home to parents describing the various opportunities available to students.

▶ Honor school staff who volunteer with youth programs.

In the Community

▶ Publicize youth programs in many different ways—through the media, posters, community bulletin boards, Web sites, etc. Often youth don't participate because they aren't aware that programs exist.

▶ Use discounts, special promotional offers, and giveaways to attract young people to youth programs.

▶ Make programs accessible. Try to locate them on bus lines and/or in neighborhoods where the kids are. Or offer transportation to and from.

▶ Assess current programs—especially those that aren't attracting young people. Are they offering what youth really want and need, or what adults *think* they want and need?

▶ Think intergenerationally. Start and support programs that connect old and young, adults and youth, teenagers and children.

▶ Volunteer to lead or support a youth program in your neighborhood, community, or congregation.

▶ Support school efforts to raise funds for extracurricular activities. Publish a "wish list" of equipment, supplies, etc., in the community newspaper and solicit donations.

▶ Sponsor diverse activities to reach all youth, especially those who are underserved by existing organizations.

▶ Honor community members who volunteer with youth programs. Feature stories about them in local newspapers.

In the Congregation

▶ Coordinate youth program activities so they don't conflict with important extracurricular activities. *Example:* If many members of your youth group play baseball in the spring, try to work around their practice and game schedules.

▶ Encourage youth to get involved in community groups, as participants and as leaders.

▶ Encourage adult members to volunteer as sponsors for extracurricular activities.

▶ Regularly contribute to community youth organizations.

▶ Offer to sponsor an organization or club for young people, or give an existing organization a home. Many scout troops are sponsored by local congregations.

ASSET #19

Religious Community

Kids spend one or more hours each week in religious services or participating in spiritual activities.

| **64%** | *of the youth we surveyed have this asset in their lives.* |

At Home

▶ Choose a congregation wisely. When you find one that emphasizes your family's values, your children are more likely to internalize those values and make responsible decisions.

▶ As much as possible, allow your kids to share in the choice about where to attend religious services. Or, if more than one service is offered, perhaps they could choose the time.

▶ Encourage active involvement in religious activities by modeling active involvement. Don't just drop your kids off for services or classes and pick them up later.

▶ Incorporate faith and spirituality into your daily life. Choose ways that best fit with your values and traditions.

▶ When making important family decisions, consider them within the context of your faith.

▶ Volunteer to lead or assist with a religion class for young people.

At School

▶ Don't schedule school activities that conflict with important religious holidays, and be sure to consider the many different faith traditions within your school population (students and staff).

▶ Communicate with local religious organizations. Share holiday and activity schedules. Try to coordinate with as many as possible to avoid scheduling conflicts.

▶ If possible, incorporate information about religious holidays and traditions into class discussions. Be sure to check with your school policy first, since this is not permitted in some schools.

In the Community

▶ Don't schedule community activities that conflict with religious holidays, and be sure to consider the many different faith traditions within your community.

▶ Include religious youth workers on community-wide youth councils and task forces.

▶ Partner with local congregations in sponsoring community-wide youth events.

▶ Sponsor a series of presentations on the different faiths in your community. Invite representatives from the various religious organizations to speak. Publicize the presentations.

▶ Post congregational activities involving youth on local cable channels and electronic bulletin boards.

In the Congregation

▶ Develop strategies for your youth program that address the concerns, needs, interests, and issues of young people in your congregation.

▶ Emphasize programming that keeps youth involved in the congregation throughout high school.

▶ Include youth representation on your board.

▶ Start a suggestion box for young people. Invite them to contribute their ideas for youth activities, programs, and special events.

▶ Don't lose touch with youth over the summer. Maintain year-round connections and programs that will keep them interested and involved.

ASSET #20
Time at Home

Kids go out with friends "with nothing special to do" two or fewer nights each week.

> **50%** of the youth we surveyed have this asset in their lives.

At Home

▶ Set limits on how often kids can go out with their friends during the school week. Have a family meeting to determine what seems reasonable and fair, starting with a basic guideline of four nights at home.

▶ Be firm about the four nights at home, but not inflexible. Encourage your children to get involved in creative activities, youth programs, and service to others. Make a distinction between having "something specific to do" and having "nothing special to do."

▶ Make time at home fun for everyone. Spend time together doing things you all enjoy. Play favorite games, have a family video night, read, take walks or bike rides.

▶ Monitor where your children go and who they're with, even when they're teenagers.

▶ If your teenager has a part-time job, limit it to 15 hours a week or less during the school year. Studies have shown that teenagers who work more than 15 hours a week have more problems than those who work fewer hours.

▶ Allow your children to invite friends over on some of their "at home" nights. *Examples:* Maybe the science study group could meet at your house, or your kids' friends could gather to watch videos.

▶ Limit the amount of time your children spend at home alone. Plan to be home with them as much as you can. Sit down to dinner together. Be available to help with homework or just talk.

▶ Make your home a warm and inviting place for all family members—somewhere your kids want to be. If you feel that family members argue too much or have trouble communicating, seek outside help. Family counselors are expert in helping families to get along better.

At School

▶ Limit the number of nights per week that students can be involved in school activities. Train adult leaders to help kids set priorities.

▶ Encourage coaches, club sponsors, and others not to overschedule students.

▶ Spread special school events over the whole school year instead of grouping them around holidays or other occasions.

In the Community

▶ Limit the number of nights youth are expected to participate in activities.

▶ Create community calendars that include all different kinds of youth activities—in schools, congregations, community organizations, etc. Distribute them widely (through a community newspaper, cable access, or a community Web site) so families can plan and set priorities together.

▶ Sponsor workshops for parents on communicating with kids. Offer suggestions for activities and projects families can do together.

▶ Limit the number of evenings adults are expected to participate in activities and meetings so they can spend more time at home with their children. Reinforce the importance of spending time at home.

In the Congregation

▶ Encourage families to schedule regular "family nights." Offer suggestions for activities and projects to do as a family. Include ideas in worship bulletins and mailings to member households.

▶ Limit the number of evenings youth are expected to participate in activities related to your youth program.

▶ Limit the number of evenings adults are expected to participate in activities, meetings, and committees so they can spend more time at home with their families.

Tips for Teens: Build Your Own Assets

Asset #17: Creative Activities

GOAL: To spend three or more hours per week in lessons or practice in music, theater, or other arts.

Participating in the arts–*any* of the arts–is a great way to develop your creativity, make new friends, master new skills, boost your brain power, and strengthen your self-esteem. Plus it's challenging, stimulating, rewarding, and fun. It feels good to be around art, and it feels even better to *make* art.

If your school offers classes, clubs, and after-school programs in music or the arts, you're lucky; many schools don't. Take advantage of these opportunities while they're available to you. If you'd love to play the saxophone but you can't afford to buy one, tell your teacher. Schools with music programs often have instruments available to borrow or rent. If that's not an option, ask for donations from community groups. Contact local newspapers and ask them to write stories about your school's search for musical instruments . . . or art supplies, lighting equipment for the drama club, a portable stereo system for the dance club, or whatever else you need.

Check with community education and arts organizations to see what's available there. You may find free or low-cost courses on calligraphy, photography, drawing, tap dance, singing, or playing the violin. Do your parents have talented friends? Maybe they can give you lessons in their specialties.

If your parents offer to pay for lessons, say yes . . . unless your dreams differ from theirs. *Example:* They want you to play classical piano; you want to play jazz trumpet. Talk with them about your dreams. Ask for their help and support. You might propose a compromise: If they'll pay for this year's trumpet lessons, you'll study piano next year.

Keep in mind that it's less important to become a great performer (or painter, or writer) than it is to enjoy and appreciate what you do.

Asset #18: Youth Programs

GOAL: To spend three or more hours per week in sports, clubs, or organizations at school and/or in the community.

If you're not thrilled by any of the teams, clubs, or organizations offered at your school, are you sure that you've checked into all of them? You may find a special interest group you enjoy. If not, think about starting one. Find five to ten other students who share your interest, then get together and talk about the kind of group you'd like to start. Once you've defined your purpose, decided on a few goals, and outlined some possible activities, approach a teacher you like and ask him or her to sponsor you.

Learn what's available for youth at your community center, local arts organization, and religious community. Find out what civic groups offer. You'll probably discover groups especially for young people, and groups of adults that welcome young people. If you don't find something that interests you, post messages on bulletin boards. You'll find other people who share your interests, and you can decide together what to do next.

Asset #19: Religious Community

GOAL: To spend one or more hours per week in activities in a religious institution.

Your congregation can be a source of support, encouragement, and affirmation throughout your life. A faith community of caring people who share similar values and views can be a good place to find adults to talk to—just what you need to build asset #3.

Many kids drop out of their congregations as teenagers. Organized religion no longer seems relevant to their lives. Their parents may want them to keep attending services, but eventually they decide that it's not worth arguing about. If you feel that your congregation is out of touch with young people, don't drop out. Speak up. Talk with the people who lead the youth program. Come with ideas and offer to help. Suggest a roundtable discussion—an opportunity for young people to express their opinions, thoughts, and needs.

Don't just expect your religious community to serve you. What can you contribute? *Example:* If you'd like your place of worship to offer one service a month especially for young people, maybe you could help to organize it. The more involved you become, the more meaningful the experience will be for you, and the less likely you are to walk away.

If your parents aren't involved in a religious community, this doesn't mean that you can't be. Perhaps you can join a friend's congregation. Or visit the congregations in your neighborhood or nearby. Talk with the people who lead the youth program and explain that you're looking for a congregation to join.

What if your parents are involved in a religious community, but their choice doesn't seem right for you? Try talking with them about the way you feel. Maybe they will agree to help you find a community that meets your spiritual needs.

Asset #20: Time at Home

GOAL: To spend two or fewer nights each week out with friends "with nothing special to do."

If your parents don't limit the amount of time you can spend away from home, try setting your own limits. Focus more on your school work and your family, and see if your life changes in positive ways.

For young people with jobs, spending time at home seems less important than putting in the hours at work. But when researchers at a university in Pennsylvania studied 1,800 high school students, they learned that those who work more than 15 hours a week have more problems than those who work fewer hours. Their school work suffers. Their grades fall. They don't score as well on achievement tests.

You may not have a choice; you may have to work more than 15 hours a week to help support your family. In this case, you're doing the best you can under the circumstances. But if you do have a choice, keep your hours to a minimum.

Building Internal Assets

Commitment to Learning

Young people need to develop a lifelong commitment to education and learning.

The more committed a child is to learning, the more likely it is that he or she will grow up healthy.

The commitment to learning assets are:

21. Achievement motivation
22. School engagement
23. Homework
24. Bonding to school
25. Reading for pleasure

ASSET #21

Achievement Motivation

Kids are motivated to do well in school.

> **63%** *of the youth we surveyed have this asset in their lives.*

At Home

▶ Clearly communicate to your children that you value learning—that you think school is important, and you want and expect them to take it seriously.

▶ Model lifelong learning. Show an ongoing interest in learning new things, making new discoveries, and exploring new topics.

▶ Stay in contact with teachers about your children's progress in school. Don't wait for report cards.

▶ Encourage motivation from the *inside out*. Tap into your child's interests and passions, and try to connect them to what he or she is learning in school. Don't "pay" your child to learn with money, rewards, or excessive praise; that's motivation from the *outside in*.

▶ Learn along with your children. Go someplace new together and explore. Read the same books and discuss them afterward, or take turns choosing books for everyone to read. Take a community education class together. Brainstorm a list of questions you're all curious about, then visit the library to find the answers.

▶ Encourage your kids to do their best at school, but don't expect perfection, and leave room for mistakes.

▶ Relate what your child is learning in school to real-life situations. *Example:* Visit your state's capital when your child is studying state capitals.

▶ If your kids seem apathetic about school or resist going to school, try to find out why. Is school too easy for them, or too hard? Are they getting the help and support they need? Do they feel safe at school? Talk with their teachers. Do what you can to change things, working with other parents and school staff– or switch schools.

At School

▶ Relate lesson content and curricula to real-life situations and issues. Use enrichment materials.

▶ People learn in different ways. Train teachers to recognize and teach to various learning styles, and to value the many different kinds of intelligence.

▶ Affirm and encourage achievement in diverse areas as students discover their own interests and capabilities.

▶ Encourage teachers to get to know their students. Personal attention and interest from a teacher can be powerful motivators.

▶ Honor and affirm students who do well in school. Award academic letters–like athletic letters–in official ceremonies. Feature star learners on bulletin boards along with star athletes. Encourage the media to report on your academic achievers.

In the Community

▶ Make sure that your programming for youth is enjoyable, meaningful, and intellectually challenging. Sponsor trips to museums, exhibits, films, lectures, etc.

▶ Encourage young people to use what they're learning in school to address issues in your youth program. For example, if they have been studying cultural diversity, they might have good suggestions for making your program more inclusive.

▶ Put motivated, achieving high school students together with younger kids on community projects. The older kids might inspire the younger ones.

▶ Start a Speakers' Bureau of high achievers in your community—including both adults and students. Publicize their availability to speak at area schools.

▶ Volunteer to be a tutor or a mentor in a school. Show that you value learning by donating your own time and expertise.

In the Congregation

▶ Affirm the value of education in all youth programming. Even if you disagree with the way a particular subject is taught, address that subject only; don't undermine education as a whole.

▶ Make school a regular topic of conversation in youth groups.

▶ Make youth programming intellectually challenging. Help young people to see, appreciate, and think about the complexities in faith, theology, and ethics. Affirm kids who ask tough questions. When appropriate, have them apply skills they learn in school to the content of your youth program.

ASSET #22
School Engagement

Kids are actively engaged in learning.

64% *of the youth we surveyed have this asset in their lives.*

At Home

▶ Talk with your children about school and learning. Ask them every day what they did in school, what they learned, what they liked about school, what they didn't like about it. Stay in touch with their school experience.

▶ Make learning a family affair. Learn more together about your children's favorite subjects. Involve them in your hobbies and interests. Learn a new skill together.

▶ Help your children stay alert in school by ensuring that they eat well and get enough sleep.

▶ Make it a point to attend school conferences and special events.

▶ Help your kids explore all the options available at their school. They may not be aware of interesting opportunities.

▶ Provide a positive learning environment in your home. Limit TV-watching time; have books, magazines, and newspapers available; eat dinner as a family and discuss current events.

▶ Take it seriously when your child expresses boredom or frustration with school or mentions other problems (even small ones). Talk with the teachers right away.

▶ Model lifelong learning. Take classes in your own areas of interest and talk to your kids about them.

At School

▶ Conduct an "Interest Survey" at the start of the school year to find out what your students are interested in. Give them opportunities throughout the year to work on projects related to their interests.

▶ Actively engage your students with a variety of teaching methods. Appeal to all of their senses; teach to every learning style.

▶ Tie classroom learning to students' real-life situations, issues, and concerns. Draw connections between what they're learning in school and what's happening in their lives, in the community, and in the world; invite them to do the same.

▶ Start an after-school or lunchtime discussion group where students can talk about issues, concerns, problems, fears, hopes, and dreams.

▶ Ask students to evaluate their own learning experiences. Ask what they need to feel more engaged in and excited about school.

▶ Make your classroom a warm and welcoming place to be.

▶ Honor or reward teachers who are particularly effective in keeping students engaged in learning. Have students nominate and vote for a "Teacher of the Year."

In the Community

▶ Ask youth you meet and talk with how they're doing in school. Encourage them to do well. Talk positively about your own school experiences.

▶ Work with the schools to develop lesson plans and curricula that relate to your community. *Example:* Is your town working to save a local stream? Preserve a historic site? Build a new library? Lessons related to these topics can link learning to real life.

▶ Offer community education classes for the whole family.

▶ Volunteer in a school as a tutor, club leader, reader to young students, or other helping role.

▶ If your business employs youth, show genuine interest in their school performance. Encourage them to do well in school. Limit their work hours to no more than 15 per week—fewer during finals.

▶ Counter messages in the media that describe school as meaningless or boring.

In the Congregation

▶ Tie activities in the congregation to topics young people are studying in school.

▶ Survey youth about which topics they would like to learn more about. Invite experts in to teach and talk.

▶ Use a variety of learning and teaching methods in religious education settings. Ask the teachers in your congregation for ideas and suggestions. Learn about learning styles.

▶ Be a learning congregation. Discuss sacred writings as an entire congregation; form intergenerational groups to discuss specific topics; visit local art museums to view religious paintings and scuplture.

ASSET #23
Homework

**Kids do at least one hour of homework
every school day.**

> **45%** *of the youth we surveyed
> have this asset in their lives.*

At Home

▶ Provide a quiet, comfortable, well-lit place for your
kids to study without distractions. Together with your
child, set boundaries about interruptions (phone calls,
visitors, etc.).

▶ Work with your child to set up a regular homework
schedule, then respect it. Arrange dinner and family
events around the homework schedule.

▶ Start a home reference library and keep it current.
Begin with the basics: dictionary, thesaurus, almanac,
desk encyclopedia, atlas. Add reference books on
specific topics of interest to your child. If you have a
home computer, consider purchasing an encyclopedia
on CD-ROM; these are very affordable, especially
when compared with traditional sets of encyclopedias. An Internet connection gives your kids access
to vast amounts of reference materials and homework help.

▶ Turn off the television and limit the hours your teen
can spend at an after-school job. *Tip:* Experts recommend no more than 15 hours per week.

▶ If homework time comes before dinner, make healthy snacks available. Hungry kids have trouble concentrating.

▶ Be available to answer questions, drill on vocabulary words, check homework, and offer support. Or study together; while your child does schoolwork, read, study something new, or catch up with some work.

▶ Help your child to prioritize homework assignments. (It's best to do the hard ones first—to get them out of the way before fatigue sets in.) Work with your child to plan long-term assignments.

▶ Monitor homework. Don't hover, but do check in with your child every so often and ask "How's it going?"

At School

▶ Regularly assign homework and hold students accountable for completing it and turning it in.

▶ Communicate with other teachers about homework, test schedules, and long-term assignments. Spread them out evenly over the year so students aren't swamped.

▶ Make homework relevant to other parts of students' lives—family, work, hobbies, community.

▶ Set up a homework hotline staffed by teachers, other adults, and older students. If your school is online, start a homework help chat room or bulletin board.

▶ Teach students how to use the library and the Internet to find reference materials and homework help.

In the Community

▶ Arrange after-school study programs. Set aside a quiet room for kids to do their homework, read, study for tests, etc. Staff it with adult mentors and tutors from the community.

▶ Expect young people to complete their homework as a requirement for participating in activities and programs. You won't be able to monitor this, but you can ask kids if they are keeping up with their homework and encourage them to do so. If enough adults express interest and concern, this becomes a community standard.

▶ Schedule a "homework hour" before after-school or evening activities.

▶ Set up a homework hotline staffed by volunteers from the community. Encourage the local high school to adopt this as a service project; give students service credits for working the hotline on school nights and weekends. Provide resources: telephones, desks and tables, dictionaries, computers, reference works (including, if possible, current editions of encyclopedias on CD-ROM), Internet connections, etc.

In the Congregation

▶ Reduce conflicts between time commitments for religious activities and homework. Try not to overschedule youth group members during the school year. Plan weeknight activities for later in the evening, after homework is finished.

▶ Set up a homework hotline staffed by adults and high school students from the congregation.

▶ Open the youth room after school as a study and homework center. Staff it with adult volunteers.

ASSET #24
Bonding to School

Kids care about their school.

> **51%** *of the youth we surveyed have this asset in their lives.*

At Home

▶ Part of bonding to school involves knowing that someone in school cares about you. Tell your child about one adult and one peer in your school who cared about you. Ask your child which adult and which friends he or she likes best at school and why.

▶ Encourage your child to participate in activities that boost school spirit.

▶ Set up a school bulletin board in a prominent place in your home. Post the school calendar and school notices. Meet once a month to choose which school activities to attend as a family.

▶ Encourage school pride by buying T-shirts, sweatshirts, caps, or other clothing with the school's name or logo for your child to wear. Display a school bumper sticker or window sticker on the family car.

▶ Call the school and see if you can subscribe to the school newspaper through the mail. When it arrives, read it and discuss it with your child.

▶ Invite a teacher to go out for breakfast, lunch, or coffee with you and your child. Invite a teacher to dinner at your home.

▶ Write thank-you notes, leave voicemail messages, or send email notes to teachers and administrators when you're pleased about something at your child's school.

▶ Listen to your children when they complain about school or talk about not feeling connected to school. Is there a specific problem that should be addressed? Take any concerns to your child's teachers. Be calm and respectful.

▶ Show that *you* care about your child's school. Join a parent-teacher organization; attend school conferences and special events; volunteer as a tutor, club advisor, or parent helper.

At School

▶ Provide many opportunities for students to celebrate and boost school spirit. *Examples:* Have a schoolwide contest to choose a new school slogan, T-shirt motif, song, or cheer. Decorate bulletin boards and walls with school spirit slogans and symbols. Have each classroom or homeroom design its own banner. Give monthly "School Spirit Awards" to the most caring, enthusiastic, and involved students, teachers, administrators, support staff members, and volunteers.

▶ Produce school T-shirts, sweatshirts, caps, jackets, buttons, and other items so students can wear visible signs of their school affiliation.

▶ Provide many opportunities for parents (and other adults) to volunteer at school. Volunteering encourages parents to care about their kids' school, and their enthusiasm gets passed along to their children.

▶ Make sports, arts, drama, band, choir, and other school programs inclusive so all kids can participate.

▶ Invite alumni to write articles for the school news-paper, yearbook, or Web site about what the school has done for them.

▶ Don't limit school spirit to one type of activity (typically sports). Celebrate many strengths in your school.

In the Community

▶ Support school fund-raising efforts (*examples:* bond issues, candy sales), read-athons, and teams.

▶ Attend school performances, plays, and concerts.

▶ Recognize entire schools or classrooms. Reward students for good attendance.

▶ Highlight school accomplishments in the local media, at civic gatherings, and anywhere else you can think of.

▶ Have students share their school experiences with community leaders and groups.

▶ Never allow the quality of schools to suffer because of a lack of financial resources.

In the Congregation

▶ Give young people opportunities to talk about their school experiences. Your congregation might include youth from many area schools. Sharing can help them to connect with each other and communicate pride in their schools.

▶ Encourage adult members to attend school activities involving youth from your congregation. Announce them in the bulletin or newsletter.

ASSET #25
Reading for Pleasure

**Kids read for pleasure
three or more hours per week.**

24% *of the youth we surveyed
have this asset in their lives.*

At Home

▶ Model reading for pleasure. Talk with your children about what you're reading; make your enthusiasm for reading obvious to them. Explain how reading gives you pleasure while helping you learn about life and the world.

▶ Set aside a regular family reading time each day or week.

▶ Make reading aloud a family activity. Read to your kids as long as they'll let you. When they're old enough, take turns reading out loud to each other.

▶ Give your kids access to many different types of reading material: books, newspapers, encyclopedias, almanacs, magazines. Give each other books and magazine subscriptions for birthdays and holidays. Put bookcases in your children's rooms so they can fill them with their favorite books.

▶ Pay regular visits to the library. Children who are old enough to write their names should have their own library cards.

▶ Limit television watching.

▶ Read the same books as a family and talk about them afterward. Let your children choose some of the books your family reads.

▶ Play word games (Scrabble, Boggle) together. Put magnetic words and letters on the refrigerator and write messages and poems to each other.

▶ When a movie based on a book is released (and it's something your family wants to see), read the book first. Then go to the movie together or rent the video. Afterward, talk about how the two compare.

At School

▶ Provide quiet time during the school day for students to read—and a cozy corner of the classroom where they can go. Let them choose what they want to read.

▶ Make many types of books available in the classroom—fact-filled almanacs, books of quotations, story books, picture books, reference books, and more.

▶ If some kids don't like to read or have difficulty reading, let them listen to books on tape.

▶ Have students write book reviews for the school newspaper or Web site. They might also give brief reviews over the morning announcements or your school's closed-circuit TV network.

▶ Feature fun books in the library. Form a student committee to read and recommend books.

▶ Pair younger students with older students who love to read.

▶ Help students to write their own books; start a classroom library of student-created books.

In the Community

▶ Emphasize the importance of reading by volunteering to read to children at schools, libraries, community centers, recreation centers, parks, etc.

▶ Have a community-wide read-athon. Reward students who participate with a congratulatory letter from the mayor or a local celebrity.

▶ Donate quality books and books on tape to schools, libraries, bookmobiles, child-care centers, and other places young people spend time.

▶ Make sure that your local libraries are adequately funded and staffed. Keep them open after school and on weekends.

▶ Encourage bookstores to feature great books for kids.

▶ Start "Frequent Reader Clubs" for students of all ages, with incentives for participating. Promote the clubs with posters and flyers in area businesses and places where kids hang out.

▶ Have a community-wide drive to gather used books, then donate them to needy families and/or shelters.

In the Congregation

▶ Create a library and reading room for youth in your congregation. Keep it stocked with all kinds of books that might interest them (ask for their suggestions).

▶ Include current books for kids in the congregation's library.

▶ Have youth serve as readers during services.

▶ Refer to books in sermons and religious education classes.

▶ Invite kids to write book reviews for the newsletter on books that relate to issues or concerns in the congregation.

Tips for Teens: Build Your Own Assets

Asset #21: Achievement Motivation

GOAL: To be motivated to do well in school.

Do you feel as if school is a waste of your time? You can do something about it. Take charge of your education. Set goals for yourself, ask questions in class, and find an ally–a teacher or school counselor who can help you get more out of school.

Consider your friends' attitudes toward school. If you're spending most of your time with kids who hate school and do the minimum work needed to pass, maybe you need new friends.

School success is your ticket to a good job, college or trade school admission, scholarships, financial aid, and other important steps toward becoming independent and achieving your goals. If your grades could use some help, see what's available at your school. Can you get a tutor? Can you ask your teachers for tips on raising your grades?

Often, grades are a combination of factors: assignments done, papers turned in on time, test scores, class participation. Don't make the mistake of skipping assignments or turning papers in a day late. What seems to you like an insignificant little worksheet can affect your final grade.

Asset #22: School Engagement

GOAL: To be actively engaged in learning.

You'll spend 13 years of your life in school—longer if you continue your education in college, trade school, and graduate school. You can view school as a prison sentence or an adventure; it's up to you. Your teachers can try to inspire you; your parents can try to encourage you; but what you get out of school depends on *your* attitude, *your* enthusiasm, *your* willingness to learn.

If you're already excited about school, that's great. If you're not, how can you get excited? What can you do to make learning more interesting and enjoyable? Even in the dullest, deadliest class, you can probably find *one* thing that sparks your interest. Pursue it. Try to relate what you're learning to real life. Tell your teachers (and your parents) that you want to become more engaged in your own learning. Ask for their support and suggestions. Make the effort to stay awake in class (*tip:* sit up front, if possible) and keep up with the assignments. Ask questions if there's something you don't understand. Participate in class discussions. Deepen your understanding of a subject by doing a special project or interviewing an expert. Investigate something you're curious about. Come up with your own ideas and try them. You have nothing to lose and much to gain.

Asset #23: Homework

GOAL: To do at least one hour of homework every school day.

Make homework your first priority—before favorite TV programs, time with your friends, extracurricular activities, even a job. What if you don't have at least five hours of homework in a typical week? Spend the time reading more about a particular subject, practicing your skills, or reviewing your books and notes. It's vital to form the homework habit *now*, especially if you plan to go to college.

If you have a part-time job during the school year, limit your work schedule to 15 or fewer hours per week to allow time for homework and other activities that are important to your overall development.

Asset #24: Bonding to School

GOAL: To care about your school.

If you're feeling disconnected from your school—tuned-out, bored, uninterested, as if it's just a place you have to go—talk to a parent, teacher, school counselor, or other adult. Work together to identify ways you can feel more connected.

You might start by identifying one thing you like about your school, then get involved. Or identify one thing you like to do, then find out if your school offers anything—a course, a club, a team—that matches your interest. If it doesn't, start something. Find an adult sponsor (usually a teacher) who's willing to support you. Write a proposal for your club and present it to the principal, faculty, or club coordinator at your school. Then advertise your club to attract new members.

Brainstorm ways to boost school spirit in yourself and other students. What about having a schoolwide contest to design a school symbol or create a school slogan? Could your group or club create inspiring banners for the halls? Are there good things happening at your school that the community should know about? Maybe you could write news releases for the media.

If your school has serious school spirit problems—if most students seem disconnected or apathetic—find a school in your community where school spirit is strong. Learn what they're doing differently. Talk with teachers, administrators, and student leaders. Bring some of their ideas back to your school.

Asset #25: Reading for Pleasure

GOAL: To spend three or more hours per week reading for pleasure.

Don't underestimate the importance of reading. It's vital to your current and future success. The more you read, the stronger your reading skills will become. Skilled readers perform better on tests, read more quickly and easily, and get more out of what they read. They're more likely to ask questions when they don't understand something; to look up words they don't know; and to take notes on what they read.

If you haven't formed the reading-for-pleasure habit, it's not too late to start. Think of something—anything—you'd like to know more about, then visit the library. Ask the librarian to help you find a book or magazine on that topic. Once you've read that, read another. Or search the Internet for articles that interest you. Three hours per week of reading may sound like a lot, but it's less than 26 minutes a day. (So skip a sitcom.)

To give yourself and your friends an extra push toward reading for pleasure, consider starting a book club. Decide each month on a book you'd all like to read and set a deadline for reading it. Afterward, get together and talk about it.

Positive Values

Young people need to develop strong values that guide their choices.

The more a child develops positive values that guide her or his behavior, the more likely it is that she or he will make positive choices and grow up healthy.

The positive values assets are:

26. Caring
27. Equality and social justice
28. Integrity
29. Honesty
30. Responsibility
31. Restraint

ASSET #26
Caring

Kids place high value on helping other people.

> **43%** *of the youth we surveyed have this asset in their lives.*

At Home

▶ Regularly spend family time helping others. Volunteer at your local food shelf, at shelters or soup kitchens for homeless people, at nursing homes. It's tremendously inspiring for kids to see their parents helping others and to know that they can make a difference, too.

▶ Show care and concern for your neighbors. Is there an elderly person who needs help with shopping and home maintenance? Someone who could use a hand with yard work? Set a good example and get your kids involved.

▶ Have family meetings to brainstorm ways of helping people. Decide together that you'll spend a certain number of hours each week serving others.

▶ Instead of spending money on holiday gifts for each other, identify a family in need. (Ask at your child's school, at your community center, and/or at your place of worship.) Then work together as a family to compile a list of gifts and necessities and shop for them. Arrange to have everything delivered anonymously.

▶ Establish an atmosphere of mutual caring and help-fulness within your home.

▶ Encourage and support your teen to help other people, even when it feels uncomfortable or risky. For example, it may seem risky to do a cleanup project in a high-crime neighborhood, but if appropriate precautions are taken, the benefits for everyone can far outweigh the risks.

At School

▶ Encourage all students to participate in service activities or service-learning classes. Give credits, not grades, for participation. Work with your community to learn where students can be of the most service, then offer a range of options.

▶ Provide cooperative learning opportunities for all students. The brightest students shouldn't always be the ones who are helping others. Work with your less able students to identify their special talents and abilities so they can be helpers, too.

▶ Create a peer counseling program in your school. Train students to guide their peers in resolving conflicts and making good decisions.

▶ Honor and affirm students who help others. Give special awards and recognition for service.

▶ Honor and affirm school staff who are active in community service. Promote them as role models. Start a mentoring program to match students with caring staff.

In the Community

▶ Include service projects and reflection as an integral part of all youth programming.

▶ Work closely with your community to identify opportunities for young people to serve others. Invite youth to brainstorm service ideas.

▶ Honor and affirm youth who serve others. Sponsor an annual awards program and publicize it in local newspapers.

▶ Identify community members who are active in serving others. Invite them to speak to young people. Encourage them to mentor young people who want to serve.

▶ Participate in neighborhood rehabilitation projects. Encourage community members and their kids to help.

▶ Form relationships with national service organizations. Invite representatives to speak in your community. Encourage community members–youth and adults–to volunteer with the organizations of their choice.

▶ Teach youth caring skills and provide ample opportunities to use them within the community.

In the Congregation

▶ Include peer helping in your youth programming.

▶ Make young people aware of the service opportunities available within your congregation. Announce them during worship services. Provide opportunities for kids and adults to serve together.

▶ Make youth aware of service opportunities in the community.

▶ Invite young people to contribute their own ideas for helping others.
▶ Honor and affirm members of all ages who help others.

ASSET #27
Equality and Social Justice

Kids place high value on promoting equality and reducing hunger and poverty.

45%	*of the youth we surveyed have this asset in their lives.*

At Home

▶ As a family, discuss your views about equality and social justice. Choose one cause to follow and help.

▶ Gather information about organizations that assist or advocate for people who are poor, starving, or suffering from inequalities. Have a family discussion to decide which one(s) your family will support. Young children can set aside part of their allowance; older kids can chip in a portion of their earnings from jobs and chores.

▶ Instead of spending money on holiday gifts, make a family contribution to a charitable organization or other worthy cause.

▶ Volunteer with your family at a soup kitchen, homeless shelter, or food pantry. Join marches and demonstrations for equality and social justice.

▶ Talk with your children about world disasters and countries where people are suffering. Watch news programs, read newspapers, visit the library, and search the Internet for more information. Is there something that touches your children personally? A war, famine, earthquake, fire, or flood? Find a way for your family to help. *Tip:* Newspapers often publish the names, addresses, and telephone numbers of relief organizations following major disasters.

▶ Take family vacations in which you expose your kids firsthand to communities in need. *Example:* If you visit Washington, D.C., don't just focus on the glamorous and exciting tourist sites. Also learn about areas of the city with serious problems.

▶ Visit museums that address issues of equality and social justice.

At School

▶ Include equality and social justice as ongoing topics in class discussions and curricula. Assign research projects on current issues and events.

▶ Invite representatives from international service, relief, and human rights organizations to speak to students. If possible, have small group discussions so students and adults can interact one-on-one.

▶ Offer a unit of study on people who have made a difference in the world through activism and service.

▶ Sponsor schoolwide emphases on particular issues and concerns, then address them in all areas of the curriculum.

In the Community

▶ Work in cooperation with the school district, scouts, or other organizations on a food drive, clothing drive, or other project that promotes equality and social justice. Encourage students to be on your city's Human Rights Commission.

▶ Give young people responsibility and leadership for service projects. Let them prove to themselves that they can make a difference.

▶ Sponsor community discussions about equality and social justice. Invite representatives from service and relief organizations to speak. Schedule the discussions for a time when kids can attend with their parents.

▶ Post fact sheets about hunger, poverty, inequality, and injustice on bulletin boards. Have brochures available from service and relief organizations.

▶ Always take time to talk with young people after they have completed service projects. This helps them to understand the issues and make important connections between their actions and how they affect others.

In the Congregation

▶ Address issues of equality and social justice in your youth programming. Sponsor discussions and arrange ways for youth to get involved.

▶ Address these issues in sermons, homilies, and messages to the congregation.

▶ Invite young people to contribute their ideas when planning ways for your congregation to address global concerns.

▶ Through trips, speakers, service projects, and simulations, make world issues personally relevant to youth.

▶ Honor and affirm members who volunteer or work for service and relief organizations.

ASSET #28
Integrity

Kids act on their convictions and stand up for their beliefs.

63% *of the youth we surveyed have this asset in their lives.*

At Home

▶ Model integrity in your daily life. Talk openly about what you believe and value, then act on what you say. When it comes to building positive values, *you* are your child's most important teacher.

▶ Have a family discussion about the meaning of integrity. Define it as simply as you can. *Examples:* being true to your convictions and beliefs; "talking the talk and walking the walk."

▶ Ask your children to articulate their convictions and beliefs. What do they stand for? What's important to them? Come up with a list of convictions and beliefs that everyone in your family shares. Post it in your home.

▶ Tell your child about a time when you stood up for something even though it was difficult to do. Explain how you felt. Then tell about a time when you *didn't* stand up for something because you were afraid. Discuss why it's easier to act on your convictions in some situations than others.

▶ Call your children's attention to times when their words and actions don't match. Encourage them to do the same for you.

▶ Celebrate when your child acts on a belief or conviction, especially when it was obviously hard to do.

▶ Whenever you notice or learn about someone who acts with integrity, point it out to your children.

▶ Comment on people's actions in the news and how they show (or don't show) integrity.

▶ Share with your children times when you're tempted to ignore your values and beliefs. *Example:* "Today a clerk gave me change for a fifty instead of a five. I could have used the extra money, but I gave it back."

▶ Affirm and support your children when they make choices that show integrity–even if they aren't the choices you'd make.

At School

▶ Include integrity in your school's stated and posted values and expectations. Look for ways to explore what it means with students of all ages.

▶ Encourage and expect all faculty and staff to model integrity.

▶ Ask students to tell in their own words what integrity means to them. Have them give examples of people who acted with integrity.

▶ Create an Integrity Bulletin Board and feature people who have acted with integrity. *Examples:* Gandhi, Martin Luther King Jr., Mother Teresa. Invite students to nominate people they know for the bulletin board– including each other. They should be prepared to explain why they are nominating someone.

▶ Highlight men and women in history and current events who acted with integrity. Find examples in literature and discuss them as a class.

In the Community

▶ Model integrity in your daily life—at home, in the workplace, in public, and wherever you go. Support and affirm youth when they act with integrity.

▶ Launch a community-wide campaign on the value of integrity. Use billboards, posters, grocery bags, flyers, local media, and the Internet to spread the word.

▶ Sponsor speeches, seminars, presentations, and roundtable discussions on the topic of integrity. Be sure to include children and teens.

In the Congregation

▶ Model integrity as individuals and as a congregation. Clearly articulate your values and beliefs and act on them.

▶ Talk about the importance of integrity within your faith tradition and sacred texts.

▶ Address integrity in sermons, homilies, worship bulletins, and mailings to member households. Give examples of people from your faith tradition (and your congregation) who have acted with integrity.

▶ Include integrity in your congregation's stated values and expectations. Make it a frequent topic in your youth programming.

ASSET #29
Honesty

Kids tell the truth even when it's not easy.

63% *of the youth we surveyed have this asset in their lives.*

At Home

▶ Model honesty in your daily life. Be honest with your children, your spouse, telemarketers, solicitors, store clerks, coworkers, friends, neighbors, relatives–and yourself.

▶ Encourage and expect family members to be honest with themselves and each other. Honestly acknowledge feelings. Honestly admit to successes and mistakes.

▶ Catch your children being honest.

▶ When you fudge the truth, admit it and apologize.

▶ Don't overreact when your child lies to you. Children will lie if they fear your reaction. If you suspect or know that your child is lying, ask "Do you think I believe you right now? Or do you think I might be having trouble believing you right now?" Give your child the opportunity to tell the truth.

▶ Have family members discuss situations they observed at work, at school, and in the community where people acted honestly and dishonestly.

- ▶ Point out when characters in TV shows and movies are being honest or dishonest. Are there any consequences for dishonesty? Do the consequences seem real?
- ▶ Point out dishonesty in advertising.
- ▶ Help your children talk through situations where it's tempting to be dishonest. Think of solutions together.
- ▶ Never punish your kids for being honest with you.

At School

- ▶ Include honesty in your school's stated and posted values and expectations.
- ▶ Establish clear boundaries and consequences for dishonest behavior (lying, cheating, stealing, plagiarism, false accusations). Publish them in the school handbook.
- ▶ Make it easier for students to be honest than to be dishonest.
- ▶ Teach honesty skills in the classroom. Have students role-play what to do and say when it's hard to tell the truth; when telling the truth might hurt someone's feelings; when they're caught telling a lie.
- ▶ Use case studies and simulations to highlight times when it's hard to be honest. Point out ways to be honest even then.
- ▶ Encourage and expect all faculty and staff to model honesty.
- ▶ Ask students to tell in their own words what honesty means to them. Have them give examples of people who acted honestly and dishonestly.
- ▶ Create a classroom display about honesty. Feature people in history who told the truth, inspiring quotations

about honesty, books about honesty, stories about honesty from newspapers and magazines, etc.

▶ Work with students to write a Code of Honesty for your classroom or school.

In the Community

▶ Make honesty a community value. Hold public officials and local celebrities to high standards of honesty. Remind them that they are role models.

▶ Notice and affirm young people who act with honesty. *Examples:* the child who returns too much change at the store; the neighborhood kid who admits to sending a baseball through your window.

▶ Feature stories in the media about people who acted honestly.

▶ Be willing to get involved when you witness dishonest behavior.

In the Congregation

▶ Model honesty as individuals and as a congregation. Be honest in your dealings with your membership, your neighbors, and your community.

▶ Make honesty the topic of sermons, homilies, articles in worship bulletins, and mailings to member households.

▶ Use sacred writings and stories to illustrate the importance of honesty.

▶ Give members a safe place to struggle with tough ethical and personal situations where honesty can be difficult.

▶ Encourage children and teens to commit to being honest together. (They might even sign an "honesty pledge" as a group.) This can be a source of strength and support when kids are pressured to cheat or be dishonest in other ways.

ASSET #30
Responsibility

Kids accept and take personal responsibility for their actions and decisions.

> **60%** *of the youth we surveyed have this asset in their lives.*

At Home

▶ Model responsibility in your daily life. When you make a commitment, follow through. When you can't or don't do something you should have, don't make excuses. Talk with your child about how you plan to avoid getting into a similar situation in the future.

▶ Keep track of responsibilities with things-to-do lists. Encourage your children to make lists of their own.

▶ Create a family chores chart and list everyone's responsibilities.

▶ Give your children opportunities to be responsible. Don't assume that a task is beyond their capabilities—but do keep your expectations realistic and allow for mistakes.

▶ Break new tasks into smaller steps and teach them one by one until your child can take responsibility for the entire task alone.

▶ Make time to teach responsibility. Don't rush your children through new tasks; don't squeeze them in when you're in a hurry or pressured to be elsewhere or doing other things.

▶ Don't nag or rescue your kids when they "forget" to follow through on a responsibility. Let natural consequences occur. *Example:* Kids who don't put their dirty clothes in the laundry basket will run out of clean clothes to wear.

▶ Recognize and affirm your child's responsible behavior.

▶ Give kids more responsibility as they mature. Keep tasks and expectations age-appropriate. If you're not sure what's suitable for your child, ask an expert or read a book about child development. *Tip:* Other parents can be experts, too.

At School

▶ Expect students to act responsibly. Notice and affirm them when they do; set clear and reasonable consequences for when they don't.

▶ Give students real responsibilities within the classroom and the school. Monitor but don't take over.

▶ Teach students how to make and use things-to-do lists.

▶ Don't assume that students know how to tackle large assignments. Show them how to break a large assignment into smaller parts, figure out what they need to complete each part, and set deadlines for themselves. Have older students teach this to younger students.

▶ Follow through on your commitments to your students.

In the Community

▶ Challenge assumptions that young people are naturally irresponsible. Call attention to ways that youth can and do act responsibly.

▶ Make responsibility a community value. Hold community leaders to high standards. Expect them to take personal responsibility for their actions and decisions.

▶ Implement a restorative justice program in your community. Don't just punish kids who break the law or violate community standards; insist that they take responsibility for their actions and repair any damage they have done.

▶ Be clear and explicit about job responsibilities for teen workers and teach them how to meet those responsibilities.

In the Congregation

▶ Give youth real responsibilities within the congregation. Assign specific tasks to children and teens and expect them to follow through.

▶ Make responsibility the topic of sermons, homilies, articles in worship bulletins, and mailings to member households.

▶ Offer workshops, seminars, and discussion groups for parents on the topic of teaching kids to be responsible.

▶ Support youth when they're in situations where it's difficult to carry out their responsibilities.

ASSET #31
Restraint

**Kids believe that it's important
not to be sexually active
or to use alcohol or other drugs.**

42% *of the youth we surveyed
have this asset in their lives.*

At Home

▶ Talk with your kids as openly as you can about sex, alcohol, and other drugs. If you're uncomfortable discussing certain topics, admit it and provide age-appropriate books. Encourage your kids to talk with other adults you know and trust.

▶ Be clear about your boundaries, values, and reasons. Most teenagers are actually *relieved* to hear their parents say "We expect you not to have sex or drink alcohol as a teenager." Explain why—and be open to questions.

▶ Invite your teenagers to make a commitment not to have sex or use alcohol during their teenage years. Many teens today are choosing to abstain, and some are going public with their decision. They're finding that this frees them from the pressures other kids experience.

▶ With your teenager, take turns stating your opinions and values on one-night stands, drinking and driving, drugs, rape (including date rape), alcohol at parties, teen pregnancy, and so on.

▶ Look for opportunities in the media (newspaper or magazine articles, TV programs, movies) to bring up the topics of sex, alcohol, or other drugs. Discuss your reaction and ask for your child's opinion.

▶ If you learn that your teenagers are already sexually active or using alcohol or other drugs, encourage them to reevaluate their choice in light of values that are important to them. *Example:* If they strongly believe in justice, talk about how having sex too early often exploits one person in the relationship. You might also seek professional guidance on how to respond appropriately.

▶ Teach and model appropriate ways to show affection. If you drink alcohol, use moderation. Never drink and drive.

▶ Tell your children that if they ever find themselves in a situation where others are pressuring them to have sex or get drunk or high, they can call you and you'll come to get them—no questions asked.

At School

▶ Give students opportunities to express their values, attitudes, and concerns about sex, alcohol, and other drugs. Start a lunchtime or after-school discussion group.

▶ Make appropriate resources (books, magazines, videos) on sex, alcohol, and other drugs available in the media center.

▶ Train peer counselors to affirm young people who choose abstinence.

▶ Work with students to create a school pledge about staying alcohol- and drug-free. Make copies available for students to sign, and inform the local media.

▶ If sex education is taught in your school, use a values-based curriculum that helps kids sort out their values and understand how those values shape their behaviors.

▶ Invite the mayor to speak at DARE graduations. Send congratulatory letters to graduates.

In the Community

▶ Support local efforts to reduce or eliminate youth access to sexually explicit movies, videos, and magazines, alcohol, and tobacco.

▶ Have clear expectations of how youth should relate to each other in all activities. Emphasize mutual respect and responsibility.

▶ Create a climate in which abstinence by youth is valued and affirmed.

▶ Invite community health professionals to speak to parents and kids about sex, alcohol, and other drugs.

In the Congregation

▶ Include discussions about restraint in your religious education programming. Clearly communicate what your faith tradition teaches about sexual behavior and the use of alcohol or other drugs.

▶ Find ways for youth to affirm and support each other in making positive choices about sex, alcohol, and other drugs. Help them articulate the reasons for their decisions.

▶ Invite young people to make a commitment not to have sex or use alcohol during their teenage years. If appropriate, they can do this publicly; if not, privately.

▶ Even if teenagers have been sexually active, encourage and affirm decisions to stop. Talk with sexually active teens about important values they can build by refraining from sexual activity.

Tips for Teens:
Build Your Own Assets

Asset #26: Caring

GOAL: To believe that it's really important to help other people.

There are many opportunities within your school, neighborhood, and community to reach out and help others. Countless young people have made (and are making) a difference in people's lives. Look around you for examples. You might have to look carefully, because children and teens who help others usually don't make a big deal about it and might not get much recognition. Ask adults you know—teachers, youth group leaders, religious leaders—to point you toward kids who are making a difference. Talk with them and ask them why they do it. You'll probably hear that the more they *give*, the more they *get* in return—respect, self-esteem, self-worth, and the satisfaction that comes from having an open hand and an open heart.

Then choose a problem you'd like to help solve. Find something that interests you on a personal level. Would you like to help homeless people? Hungry kids? A lonely neighbor? Abandoned animals? Learn more about the problem, enlist friends to work with you, brainstorm ideas, and get started.

If you're not ready to tackle a big project, you can show that you care in simpler ways. Do little acts of kindness for your family, friends, and classmates. Say something nice to or about another person. Leave a small gift or a thoughtful note in a friend's locker or on a teacher's desk. Or just smile at someone—a quick way to show you care. Decide to *be* a caring person and you'll discover that the possibilities are endless.

Asset #27: Equality and Social Justice

GOAL: To help promote equality and reduce world poverty and hunger.

We are all citizens of the world. Communication technology has made it possible to stay on top of news from almost everywhere. Turn on CNN, listen to public radio, read newspapers and magazines, and/or search the Internet to educate yourself about the world's people and problems. *Tip:* If you're online, check out the Human Rights Web *(http://www.hrweb.org/)*, a great source of information about human rights issues.

You can't stop a war or save a nation, but you can do *something*. Help to support a relief organization or human rights organization. (The oldest and biggest: Amnesty International.) Join a letter-writing campaign. Get involved with your local chapter of Habitat for Humanity, an international organization that builds homes for needy families. Volunteer at a local service organization or through your congregation. Every effort,

however small it may seem, has the potential to profoundly change someone else's life—and yours.

Asset #28: Integrity

**GOAL: To be someone who acts on your convictions
and stands up for your beliefs.**

What do you stand for? What *won't* you stand for? Are
you someone who acts on your convictions and beliefs?
How do you know? One way to find out is by making a
list of qualities that are important to you. Your list might
include honesty, honor, trustworthiness, genuineness,
and consistency. Do you have these qualities? If not,
how can you build them in yourself?

You can start by finding an adult role model—someone
you see as having integrity. This person "talks the talk
and walks the walk." It might be a parent, a teacher, a
neighbor, a religious leader, or another adult you know
and trust. Spend time together; get to know him or her.
Ask the person to tell you about times when acting on
his or her convictions wasn't easy. Share your concerns.
Examples: How can you know when to speak up and
when to stay silent? Is it always worth it to be assertive?
Can having integrity get you into trouble? What happens when your convictions clash with your parents'
convictions?

Or visit the library and look for books about
integrity. (Ask the librarian for help.) Read them and
think about them. If you're interested in exploring this
topic with friends, read the same books and talk about
them afterward.

Try to surround yourself with people of integrity—
friends who act on their convictions and stand up for
their beliefs. Then you can support each other during
tough or challenging times.

Asset #29: Honesty

GOAL: To tell the truth–even when it's not easy.

Surround yourself with friends who value honesty. These are people who don't lie about losing their homework when they just didn't do it; who don't tell their parents they're going one place when they're really going somewhere else; who don't spread gossip and rumors. Reinforce each other's efforts to be honest.

You can also make a personal commitment to tell the truth. Tell someone you trust about your commitment–a parent, teacher, close friend, youth group leader–and ask for support. Go to her or him when being honest is especially difficult for you.

When you're honest, people trust you. Adults allow you more privileges and freedom. Friends know they can count on you. You gain a good reputation because most people admire and respect honesty. You get into less trouble and feel more secure inside yourself.

Asset #30: Responsibility

GOAL: To accept and take personal responsibility for your actions and decisions.

You can accept and take more responsibility in all areas of your life. Start by brainstorming ways you can take more responsibility at home. Are there chores you could be doing? Other ways you could be helping? Could you take more responsibility for meeting your own needs? You might imagine what your life would be like if you were living on your own. Who would do your laundry? Prepare your meals? Clean your room? Manage your money? Make sure you got to school (or work) on time? How many of these tasks are your parents doing for you? How many could you do for yourself? *Tip:* Most parents notice and appreciate responsible behavior in their kids. And they tend to reward it with more privileges and freedom.

Next, think of ways you can take more responsibility at school. Then focus on your community, your friends, and your personal goals. The more responsibility you take, the stronger and more capable you'll feel.

Asset #31: Restraint

GOAL: To abstain from being sexually active as a teenager; to not use alcohol or other drugs.

Sex, alcohol, and drugs can be so tempting. Pressure to be sexually active and get high can be almost irresistible. Especially if your friends are having sex, drinking, or using drugs, you may feel left out if you aren't, too.

If you're a boy, you may think that you have to prove yourself by having sex. If you're a girl, you may feel that the only way to keep a boy interested is to have sex with him. Or you may decide that you want someone in your life who really belongs to you—like a baby. And whether you're a boy or a girl, you're probably curious about alcohol and other drugs.

Restraint requires courage—and support. Talk with your parents, teachers, youth leaders, religious leaders, and other adults you know and trust. Get the facts about STDs (sexually transmitted diseases), teen pregnancy, and what happens to kids who drink and use drugs. Think about and clarify your personal values, then surround yourself with friends who feel the way you do about sex, alcohol, and other drugs.

Abstinence is a powerful way to show that you can control yourself and you respect yourself. Even if you've already had sex, or if you've been using alcohol or other drugs, you can stop. It's not too late. Young people who have chosen abstinence report that it's a big relief. You may want to try it and see for yourself.

Social Competencies

Young people need skills and competencies that equip them to make positive choices, to build relationships, and to succeed in life.

The more personal skills a child has, the more likely it is that he or she will grow up healthy.

The social competencies assets are:

32. Planning and decision making
33. Interpersonal competence
34. Cultural competence
35. Resistance skills
36. Peaceful conflict resolution

ASSET #32

Planning and Decision Making

**Kids know how to plan ahead
and make choices.**

> **29%** *of the youth we surveyed
> have this asset in their lives.*

At Home

▶ Have family meetings to talk about plans that affect the whole family. Invite suggestions from everyone, even the youngest children.

▶ Give your teenager full responsibility for planning and preparing a family meal once a month.

▶ Model planning and decision making. Have things-to-do lists and calendars visible in your home. Give your children daily planners or datebooks and demonstrate how to use them.

▶ When your children receive long-term assignments, offer to help them plan and make decisions in order to finish on time.

▶ Give your teenager increasing responsibility for planning his or her own future. *Examples:* saving money for a special purchase; finding a summer job. Prompt good planning by asking questions, but don't take over the planning process.

▶ Model choice making: 1) gathering information, 2) viewing the choice from all sides, 3) weighing potential consequences, 4) listing pros and cons, 5) making a choice and sticking to it. Help your children apply this process to choices they're facing.

▶ Talk your children through choices. Use "what if?" questions to help them anticipate consequences. *Example:* "What if you don't clean your room by Friday when your friend comes to spend the night?"

▶ Allow for mistakes. Don't blow up at a poor choice, and don't rescue your child from the consequences.

▶ Encourage your kids to keep a journal of the choices they make. Explain that they should write down what happened *and* how they felt at the time. This reinforces good choices and serves as a strong reminder of the effects of bad choices.

▶ Point out to your children that not making a choice *is* making a choice—it's choosing not to choose. Explain that this gives someone else the power to determine what happens next.

At School

▶ Let students plan class projects, assignments, even schoolwide activities.

▶ Teach planning and organizational skills. *Example:* When you assign a research paper, assign due dates for each step—choosing a theme, doing research, preparing an outline, writing a first draft, revising, etc.

▶ Create assignment sheets for your students. Or, if your budget allows it, provide students with daily planners for the school year.

▶ Train staff to help students make long-term plans for continuing their education and choosing a career.

▶ Have students role-play making various types of decisions. Have them predict possible outcomes and consequences. Talk with them about decisions you've made and how they turned out.

▶ Ask students to talk about or write about tough choices they have made. Challenge them to articulate the reasons behind their choices.

▶ Include student leaders on decision-making committees and boards.

In the Community

▶ Have youth identify something in the community they'd like to change, then develop a plan for changing it. Take their plan seriously.

▶ Reserve room on a local cable channel for a calendar of youth activities and events.

▶ Offer workshops for community members on planning and decision-making skills.

▶ Permit young people to participate in decisions about community programs and special projects.

▶ Invite motivational speakers to talk to kids about important choices they have made.

▶ Train adult leaders to help kids through the decision-making process.

In the Congregation

▶ Give young people an active role in planning the youth program. *Example:* If kids really want a basketball court on the parking lot, have them create a plan for making it happen.

▶ Include youth in decisions that affect the congregation as a whole.

▶ Invite kids to plan special events. Even young children can do this with adult guidance and supervision.

▶ When appropriate, point out to youth how their faith informs their decisions.

ASSET #33

Interpersonal Competence

Kids have empathy, sensitivity, and friendship skills.

> **43%** *of the youth we surveyed have this asset in their lives.*

At Home

▶ Practice interpersonal skills with your child, such as meeting people, starting conversations, asking questions, and finding similar interests. Be aware that when you and your child meet new people together, your child will be watching you to see how you handle the situation.

▶ Practice seeing things from a child's perspective. Then you can truly empathize when your kids come to you with problems or concerns. You'll also be modeling empathy for them.

▶ Go to a public place with your child. Try to guess what kind of mood people are in by the way they walk and look.

▶ When your children do things that hurt other people's feelings, talk with them about how their behavior affects others.

▶ Invite people over for dinner often. Spend time as a family talking with your guests.

▶ Welcome your children's friends into your home. Spend time talking with them and getting to know them.

▶ Initiate conversations with your children about relationships. Talk about your friendships; ask about theirs.

▶ Emphasize the value of diversity in friendships. Encourage your kids to form friendships with people of different ages, ethnic origins, cultural backgrounds, and faiths. Model this in your own friendships.

At School

▶ Use role-playing and creative visualization to teach empathy, sensitivity, and interpersonal skills.

▶ Hold discussion groups about social and emotional experiences during lunch or after school. Encourage students to talk about their feelings and explore appropriate ways to express them.

▶ Expose students to the life experiences of other people in concrete ways. *Example:* When discussing the 1960s in history class, invite a Civil Rights activist to talk with your class.

▶ Use teaching styles that promote interaction and friendship-building.

▶ Mix students in groups that reflect the diversity of your school. Kids who form friendships are less likely to develop prejudices.

▶ Talk with your students about the importance of friendship in your life. Share stories and anecdotes about your friends, things you've done together, and why your friends mean so much to you.

In the Community

▶ Greet youth in the neighborhood and make time to talk with them. Get to know the family next door.

▶ Provide programs that bring children, teens, adults, and seniors together for fun and possible friendship.

▶ Emphasize cooperation over competition in activities and games.

▶ Take time to listen to kids express their feelings Encourage them to listen to each other.

▶ Make youth programs inviting and accessible to a diversity of kids (economic, ethnic, religious).

▶ Challenge youth to reach out to newcomers and others who may not have friends.

▶ Watch how youth interact with each other, and identify those who may need help with friendship skills. Train adult leaders to teach friendship skills.

▶ For activities, service projects, and special programs, mix young people in groups that reflect the diversity of your community.

In the Congregation

▶ As a congregation, model empathy and sensitivity toward each other, your community, and the world.

▶ Sponsor service projects and mission trips that bring youth into contact with different cultures and traditions. Take time to reflect on the experiences so kids will internalize the feelings of empathy.

▶ Start a discussion group on dating, making and keeping friends, and other relationship issues.

▶ Plan social events to which young people may invite friends from outside the congregation.

▶ Be a friendly congregation. Help new people and visitors feel welcome and accepted.

ASSET #34

Cultural Competence

**Kids know and are comfortable
with people of different cultural, racial,
and/or ethnic backgrounds.**

35% *of the youth we surveyed
have this asset in their lives.*

At Home

▶ Teach your children about their heritage. Encourage
them to feel proud of their cultural, ethnic, and racial
identity without feeling superior.

▶ Go as a family to events that celebrate different cultures and religions. Talk about them afterward.

▶ Include traditions from many cultures in your family
celebrations. Learn words from other languages; prepare meals from different cultures.

▶ Create a family environment that encourages positive discussion about differences. Don't tolerate jokes
or other put-downs that demean people who are
different.

▶ Expose your children to many kinds of people. Invite
friends and neighbors from various cultures and backgrounds into your home.

▶ Examine images that television, movies, and books
project of people from various cultures. Discuss what's
authentic and what's stereotypical and how you can
determine the difference.

- ▶ Encourage your child to get a pen pal from a different country.
- ▶ Check yourself for subtle racist attitudes, biases, or prejudices. Work to overcome them. Talk with your children about racism, bias, and prejudice.
- ▶ When your child has a negative reaction to a cultural or racial difference, don't ignore it. Immediately find out more about what happened and what your child is feeling. Ask questions to help your child figure out why he or she responded that way. Point out harmful, hurtful responses and suggest alternatives that promote cultural competence.

At School

- ▶ Model acceptance and appreciation of differences. Make these stated values in your school and district. Don't tolerate racism, bias, or prejudice.
- ▶ Educate teachers and other staff about respecting and working with cultural differences.
- ▶ Include the accomplishments and thinking of diverse peoples in all subjects. Incorporate information (history, literature, art, music, biography, philosophy) from many cultures into the curriculum.
- ▶ Provide activities that increase students' awareness and acceptance of differences.
- ▶ Give students opportunities to share and celebrate their own heritage.
- ▶ Teach students how to relate to people who are different from them.

In the Community

▶ Include the images and voices of a variety of people (black, white, Latino, Native American, Asian) in community publications, advertisements, posters, and promotional materials.

▶ Use local newspapers, magazines, TV, radio, etc. to educate residents about different cultures and customs within your community.

▶ Celebrate many types of cultural events within your community.

▶ Articulate clear community expectations that honor diversity and don't tolerate racism, bias, or prejudice.

▶ Celebrate your community's diversity with a heritage festival.

▶ Support and expand programs that help to deepen kids' understanding of and appreciation for their own roots. Encourage youth to embrace their heritage and claim their cultural strengths.

In the Congregation

▶ Form a relationship with a congregation that's different from yours. Provide opportunities for members of both congregations to meet, work together, serve together, and get to know each other.

▶ Make sure that the materials used in your religious education classes reflect cultural diversity.

▶ Include information and traditions from many cultures in religious education classes and worship services.

▶ Invite members of other congregations to join you for special celebrations and events. Or arrange for your youth groups to get together

ASSET #35
Resistance Skills

**Kids can resist negative peer pressure
and avoid dangerous situations.**

> **37%** *of the youth we surveyed
> have this asset in their lives.*

At Home

▶ Encourage your children to express their feelings, values, and beliefs at home. Allow them to disagree with you.

▶ Talk with your child about different ways to resist. *Examples:* Walk away from the situation; calmly say no; say how you feel; use humor; stick up for yourself (be assertive); ignore the person or situation; confront the person; call a friend to help you; stay away from the situation from then on; invite a peer mediator to help; tell a caring adult. Which does your child like best? Least? Why?

▶ Role-play with your child times when resistance skills are necessary. *Examples:* being pressured to have sex, drink alcohol, or use drugs; being asked to ride in a car with a person who has been drinking alcohol; being invited to a party at a friend's house when the parents are away; being called a coward because you won't shoplift; being called a traitor because you won't help a friend cheat on a test.

▶ Find out who your children's friends are. Get to know them.

▶ Talk with your children about peer pressure. Share stories from your own childhood and teen years.

▶ Teach your kids the difference between assertiveness, aggression, and passivity. Assertiveness is positive and affirming; aggression is negative and demanding; passivity makes one vulnerable. Role-play all three kinds of behavior with your children. Teach them assertiveness skills.

At School

▶ Encourage students to express their feelings, beliefs, values, and opinions without fear of being put down.

▶ Role-play difficult situations with students so they can practice and strengthen their resistance skills. Be open to opportunities to teach resistance skills. (See the second bullet under "At Home" on page 182.)

▶ Build resistance skills into health and prevention curricula. Talk with students about peer pressure.

▶ Train student leaders in ways to build resistance skills for themselves and their peers.

▶ Teach students the difference between assertiveness, aggression, and passivity. Model and role-play assertiveness skills. Encourage students to stick up for themselves.

▶ Show that you value assertiveness in your interactions with students—in the classroom, in teacher-student conferences, and on other occasions. Be willing to listen even when you disagree.

In the Community

▶ Provide opportunities for young people to express and act on their values and beliefs.

▶ Watch for opportunities in your encounters with kids to reinforce healthy behaviors and resistance skills.

▶ Send consistent messages to youth encouraging them to resist negative peer pressure and avoid dangerous situations. Ask the media to be partners in this effort. Ask kids what *they* think the messages should say. What language/approach is most likely to get through to kids instead of turning them off?

▶ Form teams of youth to teach resistance skills to younger kids. Use role-plays, drama, puppets, music, and art as tools in this process.

▶ Offer assertiveness training workshops and seminars for children, youth, and adults.

In the Congregation

▶ Include resistance skills in your youth education programming.

▶ Help youth to see their faith tradition as a resource in resisting negative peer pressure and avoiding dangerous situations.

▶ Role-play difficult situations with youth so they can practice and strengthen their resistance skills. Be open to opportunities to teach resistance skills. (See the second bullet under "At Home" on page 182.)

▶ Start a discussion group for young people. Encourage them to talk about times when they felt pressured to act in opposition to their beliefs.

ASSET #36
Peaceful Conflict Resolution

Kids seek to resolve conflicts nonviolently.

44% *of the youth we surveyed have this asset in their lives.*

At Home

▶ Model peaceful conflict resolution in your home.

▶ Learn and practice peaceful conflict resolution as a family. When a conflict arises: 1) Have everyone involved state their needs and wants without blaming others. 2) Have everyone really *listen* and try to understand each other. 3) Stay focused on the conflict at hand; don't bring up other conflicts. 4) Emphasize creative problem solving and new solutions. 5) Negotiate until you reach a win-win result.

▶ Allow family members to leave the discussion when they're too angry or upset to resolve the conflict peacefully. Agree on a time to reconvene and try again.

▶ Sit down together and talk about small conflicts before they become big problems.

▶ Teach your kids how to use "I-messages." The basic formula for an "I-message" is "I feel _____ when _____ because _____. I want you to _____." *Example:* Instead of "You make me so mad when you borrow my jacket without asking," your child could say "*I feel* angry and upset *when* you borrow my jacket without asking, *because* then I can't wear it. *I want you* to ask me first."

▶ Read books about peace and peaceful conflict resolution with your children. Ask your librarian for suggestions. Discuss what you read.

▶ Set up a "Peace Place" in your home. This might be a room or a corner of a room where family members can go when they need to resolve a conflict. The rules of your Peace Place might be: 1) Go there if someone asks you to. 2) Use respectful words. 3) Take turns talking and listening. 4) Use "I-messages." 5) If the problem is too big for you to solve, get help.

▶ Teach your children that hitting, pushing, kicking, and other violent behaviors are *not* okay. This goes for adults in the family, too.

At School

▶ Include peacefulness in your school's stated values. Pass a petition calling for a peaceful school and invite everyone—students, teachers, administrators, staff—to sign it. Post it where all can see it every day.

▶ Make conflict resolution training available to students, faculty and staff.

▶ Set up a "Peace Place" in your classroom. You might broaden the description under "At Home" above and make this a place where students can go anytime they want to be quiet, thoughtful, and calm. Have students decorate it with artwork and posters; make books and tapes of soothing music available.

▶ Form a Peace Club at your school.

▶ Establish a peer mediation system so students can help each other resolve conflicts peacefully.

▶ Incorporate lessons about peace and peacemakers into the curriculum.

▶ Don't tolerate violence of any kind in your school.

In the Community

▶ Develop a shared community commitment to peaceful conflict resolution.

▶ Promote and publicize the efforts of community members who are working for peace.

▶ Support programs and organizations that work to reduce domestic violence and abuse.

▶ Offer mediation services to neighborhoods, families, and youth in need.

▶ Offer classes and workshops on conflict resolution. Make them available to parents, teens, children, and whole families.

In the Congregation

▶ Teach conflict resolution skills to young people and adults. Include articles and suggestions in mailings to member households.

▶ Draw on your faith tradition's commitment to peace as you help youth build this asset.

▶ Have members share stories about times when they resolved conflicts peacefully.

▶ Establish a peer mediation system so youth can help each other resolve conflicts peacefully.

Tips for Teens: Build Your Own Assets

Asset #32: Planning and Decision Making

GOAL: To know how to plan ahead and make choices.

Some kids take life a day at a time. That's great–until they miss an important deadline, opportunity, or party.

If you're a poor planner, start simple: Make a daily things-to-do list. Number the items starting with "1" for most important. Check off items as you complete them. Move leftover items to the next day's list. Once you get the hang of this, buy a planning calendar. Inexpensive ones are available at every office supplies store. Now you can start writing in future things to do–dates of long-term assignments, school holidays, upcoming social events.

If you're a great planner, put your skills to work and help to plan something big: a school carnival, a community event, the first-ever talent show in your congregation. Keep a journal of your experience. Afterward, summarize it on a single page, with emphasis on your responsibilities. This will look very good to a prospective employer or college admissions officer.

Does it seem as if your parents make a lot of the decisions in your life, including some you'd like to make yourself? Ask if you can start making some decisions. If you prove that you're responsible, your parents will have more confidence in you. Are there some decisions that leave you feeling paralyzed? They may be too big for you to decide on your own. Get help from an adult you trust. This will give you more confidence about future decisions.

Asset #33: Interpersonal Competence

GOAL: To know how to make and keep friends.

Friendships are built on empathy and sensitivity: understanding that other people have needs and feelings, and being aware and responsive. Empathy begins by deciding how you want to be treated—probably with kindness and respect. From there, it's not too hard to understand that other people want to be treated the same. If you remember times when you were treated unkindly, even cruelly, you can make a personal commitment not to say or do things that will cause pain to others.

If you can't find friends in the usual places—school, your neighborhood, your place of worship—then look at your community as a whole. Is there a club or organization that matches one of your interests? Consider joining. You'll immediately have at least one thing in common with everyone else.

Start simply: Smile and say hi. Ask people about themselves, and tell them something about you. Invite people to do things with you—go to a movie, study in the library after school, help you with a volunteer project.

Make an effort to form friendships with many different kinds of people. Diversity makes life more interesting. Valuing and appreciating diversity—which happens naturally when your friends are different ages, races, religions, ethnic backgrounds, and genders—is an essential step toward eliminating bias and prejudice.

Asset #34: Cultural Competence

GOAL: To know and feel comfortable around people of different cultural, racial, and/or ethnic backgrounds.

If you already have this asset, you're probably enjoying the benefits. You get along with all kinds of people; you don't suspect or fear differences; you're not limited by ignorance or prejudice; and you're open to many different types of experiences.

If you don't have this asset, you're going to need it, because the world is growing more diverse each day. Here are some ways you can start building this asset for yourself:

▶ Be willing to meet new people, and make a special effort to meet people who are different from you.

▶ Watch TV shows that positively portray people from different cultural, racial, and/or ethnic backgrounds.

▶ Listen to music from other cultures.

▶ Listen when other people talk positively about friends and neighbors from other cultures.

▶ Read positive books and stories about people from many different cultures.

▶ Eat at ethnic restaurants or prepare ethnic meals for your family.

▶ Attend cross-cultural events with your family, your friends, or on your own.

▶ Choose classes and projects at school that expose you to a variety of cultures, traditions, heritages, and belief systems.

As you're learning about differences, look for similarities—the common ground where relationships are built. Overnight, your life will be more interesting, and you'll be better prepared to succeed in our changing world.

Asset #35: Resistance Skills

GOAL: To resist negative peer pressure and avoid dangerous situations.

Before you can decide what you *won't* do, you need to be clear on what you believe and why. Talk with an adult you trust about your values and beliefs. Or make a list. Start each item with "I believe. . . ." Then read your list, make any changes, and keep revising until it feels right to you. Now you know what to stick up for, say no to, and say yes to.

Resisting negative peer pressure and avoiding dangerous situations takes assertiveness skills. When you're assertive, you're firm yet respectful. You don't bully or back down. You state your position calmly and don't budge from it even when you're teased, mocked, or threatened. *Examples:* "No, I don't do drugs." "No, I don't drink." "No, I don't go to parties when parents aren't around." "No, I don't ride with drivers who have been drinking. I'll find another way home."

Don't wait until you're in a tough situation to assert yourself. Do it earlier, when the stakes aren't as high. For example, when you're trying to choose a movie with your friends, speak up about the one you really want to see.

Think of three people you can count on to be there for you and support your values and beliefs. Ask them to be your safety net—people you can call when you're pressured or tempted to do something unsafe or unhealthy. Keep their telephone numbers with you at all times. Offer to be a friend's safety net.

Asset #36: Peaceful Conflict Resolution

GOAL: To resolve conflicts nonviolently whenever possible.

If your school or community offers conflict resolution training, get involved. If there's a peer mediation program at your school, sign up. Learn everything you can about resolving conflicts peacefully. Teach what you learn to younger kids.

You can build your own conflict resolution skills. Start by thinking about a time in your past when you were involved in a major conflict. What was it about? What was your view of the situation? What was the other person's view? Were you able to resolve the conflict peacefully? Why or why not? If you got involved in a similar conflict today, would you do anything differently? Did you learn anything that might help you *prevent* future conflicts?

Role-play with your family and friends different ways to resolve conflicts. Form the habit of saying what you want, need, and feel without blaming other people. Try talking about problems *before* they grow into conflicts. Practice using "I-messages." Instead of saying "YOU make me so mad" or "it's YOUR fault" or "YOU shouldn't have done that" or "YOU always . . . ," try saying "I feel _____ when _____ because _____. I want you to _____." (*Example:* "*I feel* angry *when* we make plans to go to a movie together and you're late, *because* then we miss the beginning. *I want you to* try to be on time, okay?") Be a good listener. Look at other people when they're speaking; acknowledge what they're saying; don't interrupt, but ask questions if you need more information. Many conflicts fade away when people really *listen* to each other.

Positive Identity

Young people need a strong sense of their own power, purpose, worth, and promise.

The more a child has a sense of power, purpose, worth, and promise, the more likely it is that she or he will grow up healthy.

The positive identity assets are:

37. Personal power
38. Self-esteem
39. Sense of purpose
40. Positive view of personal future.

ASSET #37
Personal Power

Kids feel that they have control over many things that happen to them.

45% *of the youth we surveyed have this asset in their lives.*

At Home

▶ Express confidence in your children's abilities. Children who trust their own abilities have personal power.

▶ Help your children understand the difference(s) between what we can and can't control. *Example:* We can control what we say and do; we can't control what other people say and do.

▶ Encourage kids to find solutions when problems arise. Keep asking "What can you do about this?"

▶ Involve children of all ages in family decision making.

▶ Give kids age-appropriate choices at all stages of their lives.

▶ Encourage family members to point out "victim mentality comments" and "personal power comments" when family members tell about their day. *Examples:* "Sarah made me talk in class and I got into trouble" is a victim mentality comment. "Other kids teased Jacob but I didn't go along" is a personal power comment.

▶ Help family members form healthy lifestyle habits. Taking good care of oneself is an excellent way to develop personal power.

▶ Work to build social competencies in your child (assets #32–36). Kids who are socially competent are more likely to feel a sense of personal power.

▶ Encourage your children to serve others. Kids who believe they can make a difference in the world have an enormous sense of personal power.

At School

▶ Talk with students about times when they felt powerless and times when they felt powerful. What made the difference? When they felt powerless, was it because they had *no* choices? When they felt powerful, was it because they had choices?

▶ Whenever possible, give students choices—about which assignment to do, which project to work on, whether to write an essay or a poem.

▶ Reinforce the message of "the power of one" to make a difference, using real-life stories of people who have overcome adversity, spoken out, or changed the lives of others.

▶ Emphasize each student's ability to control his or her own behavior. Get help for students who have difficulty doing this.

▶ Provide a suggestion box for your classroom or school. Invite students to make suggestions for improving the school. Implement as many suggestions as possible, and recognize the students who contributed them.

▶ Actively involve students in decision making within the school. Invite their participation in determining issues of school climate, school policies, special activities, and curriculum.

▶ Help teachers find ways to maintain order in the classroom without overcontrolling their students.

In the Community

▶ Recognize and affirm young people who demonstrate good judgment.

▶ Model personal power by voting, speaking out about issues that matter to you, and being a problem solver.

▶ Include problem-solving skills in job training for teen workers.

▶ Involve youth in addressing youth issues and policies in the community. Give them useful roles and show that you value their contributions.

▶ Train adults who work with youth to affirm their abilities and give them choices whenever possible.

In the Congregation

▶ Make children and teens a vital, contributing part of your congregation by involving them in planning and decision making.

▶ Give youth a say in planning activities for the youth program.

▶ Provide young people with many options for involvement so they can choose what fits them.

▶ Provide youth with opportunities to serve others. Let them know that they have the power to make a difference.

ASSET #38
Self-Esteem

Kids feel good about themselves.

> **47%** *of the youth we surveyed have this asset in their lives.*

At Home

▶ Express your love for your children regularly and often. Show them and tell them every day how much they mean to you.

▶ Write specific things you like about your child on Post-it notes. Hide them around your child's room.

▶ Celebrate each child's uniqueness. Find something special to value and affirm, whether it's a sense of humor, computer skills, singing voice, or wonderful smile.

▶ When your kids make mistakes or bad choices, separate the deed from the doer. The *choice* is bad, not the child.

▶ Treat your children with respect. Listen without interrupting; talk without yelling.

▶ When your kids ask for something and you say no, try to give a reasonable explanation for your decision. This is common courtesy.

▶ Encourage your children to keep a journal of their accomplishments. This eventually becomes a "savings account" of positive feelings. Or keep a family "We did it!" journal. At family meetings, have family members individually name things they've accomplished, or things they've noticed other family members accomplish. Periodically celebrate these successes.

At School

▶ Use grading as an opportunity to affirm. This doesn't mean giving students grades they don't deserve. Instead, grade honestly, then add positive comments.

▶ Critique papers, reports, and tests constructively. Offer suggestions for improvements. Add positive comments.

▶ Take students seriously. Ask for their opinions; listen to their comments and suggestions; affirm their abilities and achievements.

▶ Teach students to accept criticism and respond in constructive ways.

▶ Treat all students with respect. Encourage everyone to contribute to class discussions. Identify and affirm individual talents.

In the Community

▶ Take time to pay attention to every young person— for example, while waiting in line at the grocery store or the movie theater. Demonstrate by your attitude and behavior that you value them and enjoy talking with them.

▶ Offer classes and workshops for young people on developing and strengthening self-esteem. Topics might include positive self-talk, learning from mistakes, accepting compliments, and asking for what they need.

▶ Invite experts to speak to parents about building self-esteem in children.

▶ Involve young people in planning community events. Celebrate their accomplishment afterwards.

In the Congregation

▶ Accept and affirm all young people for who they are. Recognize and affirm individual talents, abilities, and accomplishments.

▶ Hold workshops and seminars for parents on building self-esteem in their children.

▶ Feature brief biographies in the worship bulletin of young people in your congregation.

ASSET #39
Sense of Purpose

Kids believe that their life has a purpose.

> **55%** *of the youth we surveyed have this asset in their lives.*

At Home

▶ Model what it means to have a sense of purpose in life. Do things that matter to you; develop your talents; pursue your dreams. Share your sense of purpose with your children. Make it clear that you believe your life has meaning.

▶ Post inspiring quotations on the refrigerator and point them out to your children. Explain how those particular quotations affirm your values, motivate you, and help you remain purposeful. Invite your kids to find and post quotations of their own.

▶ Limit TV, computer, and telephone time. Encourage your children to use that time to develop and pursue their own interests.

▶ Have each family member list five things he or she is passionate about. Compare and discuss your family's "passion lists." Are there any surprises? If two family members share a passion, can they explore it together?

▶ Listen to your kids when they talk about their dreams. Get excited with them. Ask how you can help.

▶ Encourage your children to get involved in activities that build on their talents and interests. Network with other adults and young people who have similar talents and interests. See if you can participate in meaningful activities together.

▶ Together with your child, interview a neighbor or family member who seems to have a strong sense of purpose. How did he or she find that purpose?

▶ Give your children opportunities to find meaning in ways that are consistent with your family's values. This might involve religious activities, political involvement, service, or other pursuits.

At School

▶ Encourage students to write down their dreams and goals, both short-term and long-term. Check in with them periodically to see how it's going. Let them know it's okay to revise their goals and set new ones.

▶ Help students to see a purpose in everything they're learning in school. *Example:* Why read literature? Because it deepens our understanding of other people and ourselves.

▶ Draw connections between classroom learning and significant opportunities, needs, and issues in the world.

▶ Have students read books and stories that tell about difficulties overcome and dreams achieved.

▶ Give students opportunities to reflect on and shape their own future.

▶ Include service learning as part of the regular school curriculum. Students who make a difference in the world *know* that their lives have meaning and purpose.

In the Community

▶ Involve youth in volunteer activities. Recognize their skills and accomplishments.

▶ Invite young people you know to tell you about their dreams. Offer encouragement and advice. Be a mentor for youth whose dreams are related to your own life's purpose and areas of expertise.

▶ Provide meaningful opportunities for youth to contribute to community life.

▶ Highlight community members who have contributed to community life in significant ways.

In the Congregation

▶ Speak explicitly to kids about creating meaning in their lives and how that translates into daily activities, career choices, relationships, behaviors, etc.

▶ Encourage young people to question and develop their own values.

▶ Use religious education classes, sermons, and homilies to emphasize the importance of finding meaning and purpose in life.

▶ Help children and teens identify, nurture, and celebrate their gifts. Provide opportunities for them to build on their interests and talents.

ASSET #40
Positive View of Personal Future

Kids are optimistic about their own future.

> **70%** *of the youth we surveyed have this asset in their lives.*

At Home

▶ Inspire hope by being hopeful, optimism by being optimistic. Look forward to your future and the future of your family with joyful anticipation.

▶ Don't dismiss your children's dreams as naive or unrealistic. Instead, encourage them to tell you their dreams. Share in their enthusiasm. Help them make plans to realize their dreams.

▶ Eliminate pessimistic phrases from your family vocabulary. Replace "It won't work" with "Why not try it?" Instead of "You can't do that by yourself," try "I can help you do that."

▶ Pay particular attention to signs of hope in your community and the world. Don't just focus on all of the things that are wrong about the present or frightening about the future.

▶ Together with your children, draw pictures of your fears about the future. Talk about them . . . and then rip them up. Discuss how you have the power to deal with difficult, scary, and painful situations when they arise.

▶ Take time to enjoy life. Notice and appreciate a beautiful sunset, a good dinner, a funny show on television, a flower in your garden, a song heard on the car radio. Share your joy with your children.

▶ Be spontaneous. Drop everything to play ball, take a walk, catch a movie, or play a game with your kids. Spontaneity is essentially hopeful; you choose to do something suddenly because you expect to have a good time.

At School

▶ Encourage and support students in pursuing their dreams.

▶ Expose students to positive role models whose backgrounds are similar to theirs. This is especially important for students who come from troubled or economically disadvantaged families. It gives them hope for their own future.

▶ Create a climate of optimism. Expect your students to succeed. Even a low grade can be accompanied by an encouraging note: "I know you'll do better next time."

In the Community

▶ Help young people to set personal goals that inspire hope.

▶ Encourage kids to name their fears—things that might stop them from reaching their goals. Once fears are named, they can be addressed and dealt with.

▶ Affirm and publicize the good things about your community. Be optimistic about its future.

▶ Make a public statement about your community's commitment to the well-being of youth. Make a list of ways your community will work toward this commitment. Have it printed in your local newspaper. This will help to inspire community-wide optimism.

In the Congregation

▶ Encourage kids to talk about their hopes and dreams.

▶ Pass on to young people the hope that is integral to your faith tradition.

▶ Do projects that point to a more hopeful future. Instead of always addressing problems, identify areas of hope, creativity, and new life and encourage kids to get involved.

Tips for Teens: Build Your Own Assets

Asset #37: Personal Power

GOAL: To feel that you have control over many things that happen to you.

When you have personal power, you feel secure and confident inside yourself. You know that you have choices; you know that you can make decisions; you have a clear understanding of what you can and can't control.

If something good happens to you, you don't think "I guess I'm just lucky." You know that you somehow contributed to making it happen. Good grades don't fall out of the sky; good friendships don't form on their own. You *earn* the grades and *build* the friendships.

If something bad happens to you, you don't think "It's my fault; I deserve this; I'm a terrible person." Instead, you focus on positive steps you can take to remedy the situation.

If you believe that too many things in your life are controlled by others, you can do something about it. Talk to your parents, your teachers, and other adults who have power over you. See if they will agree to let you make more choices. Then, when you make a choice, follow through. Do what you say you will do. This shows that you're responsible and mature–someone other people can count on. And this usually leads to even *more* opportunities to choose.

Asset #38: Self-Esteem

GOAL: To feel good about yourself.

Self-talk–the messages we give ourselves–can profoundly affect our self-esteem. When you make a mistake, what do you tell yourself? "It's no big deal; everybody makes mistakes"? Or "How could I be so stupid? I can't believe I did such a dumb thing." When you succeed at something, do you say to yourself "Yes! I did it!" Or do you say "I could have done better if I really tried." In each example, the first statement is a self-esteem booster; the second is a self-esteem smasher.

Whenever you have a negative thought about yourself–when your self-talk makes you feel bad–then change it to a positive thought. Do this immediately. You'll feel better and you'll form the habit of self-affirmation, which most successful people share.

Asset #39: Sense of Purpose

GOAL: To believe that your life has a purpose.

Do you believe that your life has a purpose? If you do, then you already have this important asset. Keep strengthening it by the choices you make and the actions you take. Stay focused on your purpose and don't let anyone or anything distract you from it. On the other hand, know that people and purposes can change. Don't be locked into a goal or a dream that no longer feels right to you.

If you're not sure that your life has a purpose, or you can't figure out what your purpose might be, find some quiet time and just think. Ask yourself what really matters to you. What gets you excited about each new day? What dreams do you have for the future? What are your talents? Interests? Passions? Where would you like to be—what would you like to be doing—five years from now? Ten years from now? If you could do only *one* thing with your life, what would it be?

Questions like these can help you find a purpose, because *you do have a purpose.* No one is here by accident. Every life has meaning. If you're still not convinced—if you really, truly can't imagine why you're here—then talk with an adult you trust and respect. Try to find someone who seems to have a strong purpose in life. Explain how you feel and ask for help in finding your purpose.

Asset #40: Positive View of Personal Future

GOAL: To feel optimistic about your personal future.

What do you see when you envision your future? Are you happy or sad? In a job you enjoy or bored out of your mind? Do you have healthy, loving relationships, or are you lonely?

Studies have shown that when people picture themselves reaching their goals, they improve their chances of this really happening. The dream comes true. That's one reason why it's important for you to picture a positive future for yourself. Even if you don't know how you'll achieve the things you dream of, try to see them in your mind. Let your hope inspire you and guide you.

One way to create a positive future for yourself is to keep building your own assets. If you've been reading the "Tips for Teens" sections throughout this book, then you know which assets you already have and which ones you need to work on. The more assets you have, the better.

Roadblocks to Asset Building and How to Overcome Them

For some kids, building assets is relatively easy

When children and teens have strong families and communities—when they're surrounded by caring, loving people—not much keeps them from building assets and benefiting from the positive opportunities they encounter in life. But what about kids who don't fit this description? Some have been victimized by abuse. Others are growing up in poverty and may not have access to many positive activities and influences. Some are so bombarded with harmful influences—stress, isolation, negative peer pressure, negative values—that the positive influences can't get through.

In our nationwide surveys of youth, we also identified and measured ten roadblocks to success for young people. We call these **developmental deficits.** The more deficits a child has, the less likely it is that he or she will build large numbers of assets. As a result, the child will be much more likely to make negative decisions and choices.

The deficits are:

1. Spending two or more hours a day alone at home without an adult
2. Putting a lot of emphasis on selfish values
3. Watching more than three hours of television a day
4. Going to parties where friends will be drinking alcohol
5. Feeling stress or pressure most or all of the time
6. Being physically abused by an adult
7. Being sexually abused
8. Having a parent who has a problem with alcohol or other drugs
9. Feeling socially isolated from people who provide care, support, and understanding
10. Having a lot of close friends who often get into trouble.

A lack of economic security can also undermine efforts to build assets. How can young people benefit from music or drawing lessons if they can't afford them? What good does it do to want to go to college if you can't pay for field trips in school? How can you be alert in school if you don't get enough to eat? How can parents build a strong, caring family if they have to work two jobs just to make ends meet?

These are serious, difficult questions that we must address as a society if we really want kids to succeed. So, while we concentrate on building assets, we must also make determined efforts to prevent deficits–to break down these roadblocks to health and well-being.

How to help kids overcome deficits

Amid the bad news of deficits, there's also good news: Some young people beat the odds. Having deficits doesn't necessarily doom kids to failure. In spite of the barriers, some young people thrive. Why? Because they have important assets in their lives that balance out and even overcome the deficits.

There are five things that seem to make the most difference for young people with deficits:

1. Getting them involved in structured, adult-led activities

2. Setting boundaries and limits

3. Nurturing a strong commitment to education

4. Providing support and care in all areas of their lives, not just in the family

5. Cultivating positive values and concern for others.

While it may not be as easy for these kids to build assets, they can do it. This doesn't always involve taking them out of a difficult situation, as much as we'd sometimes like to be able to do that. It doesn't always involve a lot of money. What seems to matter most is the presence of caring people who are cheering for them, giving them opportunities, and believing in them. Kids who have this kind of support can bounce back in amazing ways and live amazing lives.

Moving Toward an Asset Mindset

We know that assets can change kids' lives

We know that when young people have enough of the developmental assets, both internal and external, they're much *more* likely to lead healthy, positive, productive lives. And they're much *less* likely to get involved in risky behaviors. Building assets in youth will free us as a society from spending so much of our time and resources on crises and problems. But first, as a society, we must move toward an asset mindset.

There's an old African proverb: "It takes a whole village to raise a child." In other words, it's not enough for young people to hear a positive message at home *or* at school *or* in the community *or* at their place of worship. They need to hear the same message reinforced in all areas of their lives. *What Kids Need to Succeed* includes ideas for parents *and* schools *and* communities *and* congregations—and teens themselves, because young people can build their own assets. Everyone has the potential to be an asset builder.

Eight ways to start building assets on your own

1. **Read (or reread) "What Do Kids Really Need?" on pages 1–18 of this book.** Look at the charts that illustrate the power of the assets to reduce risky behaviors and increase positive behaviors. Start telling other people about the importance of building assets for youth.

2. **Start reading newspaper stories about youth from a new perspective.** When you read success stories about kids, try to identify which assets are present in their lives. When you read stories about kids with problems, think about which assets might be missing for them. How can you build those assets in your community?

3. **Invite a colleague, teacher, school counselor, social worker, religious leader, or youth worker you know to meet with you.** Ask him or her to talk about his or her needs, interests, and concerns for your community. Introduce the concept of building assets in youth. Get his or her perspective. Bounce ideas around.

4. **Think about how you approach young people.** Whether you work with youth in your own family, school, community group, or congregation, do you focus more energy on intervening in crises, preventing problems, or promoting assets? How can you shift more of your energy to asset building?

5. **Share your thinking at a community meeting or event.** Give people a chance to react and talk about the potential of what you have just described. Brainstorm ways your community can work together to build assets.

6. **Affirm asset-building gestures and efforts you see others make.** Tell people that their actions are positive and powerful—that they are helping kids to succeed.

7. **Look at the list of 40 assets at least once a week and commit to at least one act of asset building every day.** Or . . .

8. **Commit to building one asset.** Choose one that's important to you and make it a priority in your life. *Examples:* You might become a mentor for a young person in your community. Or you might commit to spending more time at home with your children. Or you might undertake a family service project. Or you may decide just to be nicer to the kids in your neighborhood—to see and hear them, acknowledge and interact with them rather than ignoring them.

No one person alone can change a whole community, but everyone individually can make a significant difference.

What communities are learning about asset building

Your personal commitment is important. But it's also important that people begin thinking about how everyone *together* can build assets. How do we create neighborhoods, towns, cities, states, and even nations that put children first and make building assets a top priority? There's probably no single strategy that would work everywhere. But as communities have started asking that question, they've discovered some important principles that are shaping what they do.

EVERYONE HAS A ROLE TO PLAY

Not just parents, schools, community organizations, congregations, or governments, though they all certainly play important roles. *Everyone* can get involved in asset building. Senior citizens and children, single adults and couples, policy makers and citizens, neighbors and employers, wealthy families and low-income families, liberals and conservatives—kids need us all. And we all can share a common, hopeful commitment to kids and the future.

ASSET BUILDING IS MORE ABOUT PEOPLE THAN PROGRAMS

Relationships are the key. Quality relationships can form with or without a program—a neighbor playing basketball with the kids, a grandmother keeping an eye on the bus stop to make sure that children get off to school safely. Programs may be vehicles for connecting youth to adults, but the critical issue is the care and support that grow through relationships. Money may help sometimes, but the commitment and involvement of caring people make the most difference.

ASSET BUILDING UNLEASHES UNTAPPED RESOURCES

Most people really do care about kids; they just don't know how to express that care in tangible ways. Most communities have great services for children and families, but they're all going in so many directions that they compete and conflict with one another. Asset building gives people and organizations a clear, positive focus for their energy and resources.

ALL KIDS NEED ASSET BUILDING

Often youth programming focuses on just the "best" kids or the "worst" kids—the high achievers or the young people at risk. True, these groups may need special attention in some areas. But asset building can help *all* kids. Communities are discovering the importance of designing strategies that can benefit a broad cross-section of youth, not just a targeted few.

EVERY COMMUNITY CAN IMPROVE

Search Institute has studied hundreds of communities. While each community is different, no communities have very high levels of assets, regardless of region or size. Instead of trying to figure out who has more problems where, we all need to learn from each other.

Eight principles for getting started in your community

1. **Engage people from throughout the community.** Because the asset-building vision calls for community-wide responsibility for youth, it's important to involve many different stakeholders from the outset. A mixture of motivated citizens and their leaders provides a good balance. Many communities have developed "vision teams" with representatives from all sectors—schools, government, law enforcement, congregations, service agencies, businesses, health care providers, etc.—along with young people, parents, and other citizens, including seniors and people from various racial/ethnic and socioeconomic groups.

2. **Start with a positive vision.** The typical community-wide effort is initiated because of a crisis. Too often, however, these initiatives deal with the immediate

crisis but lack the energy or vision to sustain them. A positive vision can energize a community for the long term. It can also help groups to lay aside political and ideological agendas to work together because of their shared commitment to the well-being of children and adolescents.

3. **Build on quality information.** Many communities find that a survey of young people can be a catalyst for creative and sustained action. Quality information gives people a shared reference point for reflecting on the needs, realities, and resources in the community as they shape their vision for the future. Otherwise, you risk shaping a vision and agenda that don't adequately capture the needs, issues, and possibilities in the community for children and adolescents.

4. **Resist the temptation to create new programs.** Because most responses to youth issues in recent decades have been programmatic, intentional energy will be needed to avoid simply developing another program to respond to a specific need. The most important tasks for the "vision bearers" for asset building are to keep the vision of a healthy community alive and prompt individuals and institutions to discover ways they can integrate asset building into their own mission and commitments.

5. **Take time to motivate and educate.** Because asset building represents a new way of thinking about communities and youth, it's important not to assume that everyone automatically understands the framework and its implications. Unless people internalize the many dimensions of the asset framework, asset building risks becoming a shallow campaign to "be nice to kids." Repeating key messages about assets lays a

foundation for a more thoughtful, well-rounded response.

6. **Celebrate commitments and successes.** Asset building is a long-term vision, not a quick fix. But as communities embark on this journey, it's important to notice, celebrate, and talk about the landmarks along the way: the new awareness of young people, the shifts in conversations, the shared enthusiasm and commitments. These stories renew energy and refocus commitment.

7. **Embrace innovations from the community.** Once people are aligned with the vision of asset building, their creativity in finding ways to nurture assets can be startling. Encouraging this innovation is key to breaking out of old patterns and discovering fresh approaches to rebuilding community for kids.

   One example of grassroots innovation is occurring in Kennebunk and Kennebunk Port, Maine. Instead of being punished through the court system, first-time, nonviolent youth offenders must take a class in which they learn about what kids need to grow up healthy. In the program, called "Jump Start," each young person is paired with a volunteer mentor who lends support throughout the eight-week period. Youth who have taken the course have formed an alumni group to reinforce the positive messages they learned.

8. **Network with other communities.** While many communities have begun asset-building initiatives, the vision is still in its infancy. No one knows all the answers and no one knows how everything will work. But each community is learning something new each day. Network with others. Share stories and ideas.

Explore challenges. Together, we'll learn what works—and doesn't work—to bring the vision closer to reality.

Picturing the asset-strong community

As more communities everywhere start building assets, each community will remain unique in some ways, reflecting the personalities and priorities of the people who live there. But there are some things that likely will be in place in all asset-strong communities:

▶ Parents will have access to parent education and support that strengthens families and gives them skills in asset building.

▶ Youth programs will make special efforts to ensure that all young people are involved in positive, constructive activities.

▶ Communities will develop a consensus on what's important to them—the positive values and norms they hope to pass on to the next generation.

▶ Teens will be seen as leaders and contributors in the community.

▶ Age segregation will be minimized so that kids regularly interact with people of all ages.

▶ Youth employers, teachers, and coaches will all have training in asset building.

▶ Schools will pay as much attention to the school climate as they do to the academic curriculum.

▶ Various organizations in the community that usually operate separately from one another—government, business, schools, families, congregations—will all cooperate on behalf of kids.

There are probably dozens more good things that will occur as communities become asset-strong. Most important, people in all parts of the community will have caught the vision, joined the asset-building team, and made a commitment to helping kids succeed. When that happens, the future will indeed be brighter—not just for kids, but for everyone.

Resources for Asset Building

Almost any good book on parenting, teaching, or guiding kids contains information you can use to build assets in young people. As you become more involved in asset building, you'll probably want to visit your local library or bookstore for additional resources. What follows are brief and selective lists of titles we recommend.

Resources for Parents

Bettner, Betty Lou, and Amy Lew, *Raising Kids Who Can: Using Family Meetings to Nurture Responsible, Cooperative, Caring and Happy Children* (New York: HarperCollins, 1992).

Dinkmeyer, Don, *The Parent's Handbook: Systematic Training for Effective Parenting* (Circle Pines, MN: American Guidance Service, 1997).

Edelman, Marian Wright, *The Measure of Our Success: A Letter to My Children and Yours* (New York: HarperCollins, 1993).

Elium, Don, and Jeanne Elium, *Raising a Son: Parents and the Making of a Healthy Man* (Hillsboro, OR: Beyond Words Publishing, 1992).

Elium, Jeanne, and Don Elium, *Raising a Daughter: Parents and the Awakening of a Healthy Woman* (Berkeley, CA: Celestial Arts, 1994).

Eyre, Linda, and Richard Eyre, *Teaching Your Children Values* (New York: Fireside, 1993).

Gottman, John, *The Heart of Parenting: How to Raise an Emotionally Intelligent Child* (New York: Simon & Schuster, 1997).

Gordon, Dr. Thomas, *Discipline That Works: Promoting Self-Discipline in Children at Home and at School* (New York: NAL/Dutton, 1991).

----*P.E.T.: Parent Effectiveness Training–The Tested New Way to Raise Responsible Children* (New York: NAL/Dutton, 1985).

Guarendi, Dr. Ray, and David Paul Eich, *Back to the Family: Proven Advice on Building a Stronger, Healthier, Happier Family* (New York: Simon & Schuster, 1991).

Louv, Richard, *Childhood's Future: Listening to the American Family–Hope and Solutions for the Next Generation* (New York: Doubleday, 1992).

Metcalf, Linda, *Parenting Toward Solutions: How Parents Can Use the Skills They Already Have to Raise Responsible, Loving Kids* (Englewood Cliffs, NJ: Prentice Hall, 1997).

Nelsen, Jane, and Lynn Lott, *Positive Discipline for Teenagers: Resolving Conflict with Your Teenage Son or Daughter* (Rocklin, CA: Prima Publishing, 1994).

Schulman, Michael, and Eva Mekler, *Bringing Up a Caring Child: Teaching Your Child to Be Kind, Just, and Responsible* (New York: Doubleday, 1994).

Steinberg, Laurence, and Ann Levine, *You and Your Adolescent: A Parent's Guide for Ages 10–20* (New York: HarperCollins, 1991).

Whitham, Cynthia, M.S.W. *"The Answer Is No": Saying It and Sticking To It* (Pasadena, CA: Perspective Publishing, 1994).

Resources for Schools

Bloch, Douglas, *The Power of Positive Talk: Words to Help Every Child Succeed* (Minneapolis: Free Spirit Publishing, 2003).

Borba, Michele, and Craig Borba, *Self-Esteem: A Classroom Affair,* vols. 1 and 2 (San Francisco, CA: Harper San Francisco, 1984, 1985).

Comer, James, *Waiting for a Miracle: Why Schools Can't Solve Our Problems–and How We Can* (New York: Dutton, 1997).

Curwin, Dr. Richard, *Rediscovering Hope: Our Greatest Teaching Strategy* (Bloomington, IN: National Educational Service, 1992).

Drew, Naomi, *Learning the Skills of Peacemaking: An Activity Guide for Elementary-Age Children on Communicating, Cooperating, Resolving Conflict* (Torrance, CA: Jalmar Press, 1987).

Jalongo, Mary Renck, *Creating Learning Communities: The Role of the Teacher in the 21st Century* (Bloomington, IN: National Educational Service, 1991).

Mendler, Dr. Allen, *What Do I Do When. . .? How to Achieve Discipline with Dignity in the Classroom* (Bloomington, IN: National Educational Service, 1992).

Nelsen, Jane, and H. Stephen Glenn, *Time Out: A Guide for Parents and Teachers Using Popular Discipline*

Methods to Empower and Encourage Children (Fair Oaks, CA: Sunrise Press, 1992).

Noddings, Nel, *The Challenge to Care in Schools: An Alternative Approach to Education* (New York: Teacher's College Press, 1992).

Scales, Peter C., *Boxed In and Bored: How Middle Schools Continue to Fail Young Adolescents and What Good Middle Schools Do Right* (Minneapolis: Search Institute, 1996).

Resources for Communities

Benson, Peter, *All Kids Are Our Kids: What Communities Must Do to Raise Caring and Responsible Children and Adolescents* (San Francisco: Jossey-Bass, 1997).

Coles, Robert, *The Call of Service: A Witness to Idealism* (New York: Houghton Mifflin, 1993).

Gardner, John W., *Building Community* (Washington, D.C.: Independent Sector, 1991).

"Healthy Communities, Healthy Youth Tool Kit" (Minneapolis, MN: Search Institute, 1997).

Hechinger, Fred M., *Fateful Choices: Healthy Youth for the 21st Century* (New York: Hill and Wang, 1993).

Kretzmann, John P., and John McKnight, *Building Communities from the Inside Out* (Evanston, IL: Northwestern University Center for Urban Affairs and Policy Research, 1993).

Leach, Penelope, *Children First: What Our Society Must Do–and Is Doing–for Our Children Today* (New York: Alfred A. Knopf, Inc., 1994).

Louv, Richard, *101 Things You Can Do for Our Children's Future* (New York: Anchor, 1994).

A Matter of Time: Risk and Opportunity in the Non-School Hours (New York: Carnegie Council on Adolescent Development, 1992).

Roehlkepartain, Eugene, *Everyone Wins When Youth Serve* (Washington, D.C.: Points of Light Foundation, 1996).

Youth Service: A Guidebook for Developing and Operating Effective Programs (Washington, D.C.: Independent Sector, 1987).

Resources for Congregations

Benson, Peter L., and Eugene C. Roehlkepartain, *Beyond Leaf Raking: Learning to Serve/Serving to Learn* (Nashville, TN: Abingdon Press, 1993).

DeVries, Mark, *Family-Based Youth Ministry* (Downers Grove, IL: InterVarsity Press, 1994).

"A Foundation for Success: Congregations Building Assets in Youth" (Minneapolis, MN: Search Institute, 1998). 25-minute video.

Guy, Kathleen, *Welcome the Child: A Child Advocacy Guide for Churches* (Washington, D.C.: Children's Defense Fund/Friendship Press, 1991).

Karfield, Simon, and Amy L. Sales, *Jewish Youth Source Book: A Planning Guide for Youth Programs* (San Francisco: Brandeis University Institute for Community and Religion, 1996).

Lifegivers: A Practical Guide for Reaching Youth in a Challenging World (Nashville, TN: Abingdon Press, 1996).

Marcum, Walt, *Sharing Groups in Youth Ministry* (Nashville, TN: Abingdon Press, 1991).

Martinson, Roland, *Effective Youth Ministry: A Congregational Approach* (Minneapolis, MN: Augsburg Fortress, 1988).

Roehlkepartain, Eugene, *Building Assets in Congregations: A Practical Guide to Helping Youth Grow Up Healthy* (Minneapolis, MN: Search Institute, 1998).

Seefeldt, Glenn A., and Eugene C. Roehlkepartain, *Tapping the Potential: Discovering Congregations' Role in Building Assets in Youth* (Minneapolis, MN: Search Institute, 1998).

Varenhorst, Barbara B., *Peer Ministry Training: The Basic Curriculum* (Minneapolis, MN: Augsburg College Youth and Family Institute, 1997).

Resources for Young People

Bernstein, Daryl, *Kids Can Succeed! 51 Tips for Real Life from One Kid to Another* (Holbrook, MA: Bob Adams, Inc., 1993).

Bingham, Mindy, Judy Edmondson, and Sandy Stryker, *Challenges: A Young Man's Journal for Self-Awareness and Personal Planning* (Santa Barbara, CA: Advocacy Press, 1984).
———*Choices: A Teen Woman's Journal for Self-Awareness and Personal Planning* (Santa Barbara, CA: Advocacy Press, 1984).

The Coping With . . . Series (New York: The Rosen Publishing Group and Center City, MN: Hazelden Publishing, 1982–). Topics include feelings, health, friends, parents, self-esteem, school, the future, substance abuse, and more.

Eliot, Robert, and Dennis L. Breo, *Is It Worth Dying For? A Self-Assessment Program to Make Stress Work For You Not Against You* (New York: Bantam Books, 1989).

Kids' Random Acts of Kindness (Berkeley, CA: Conari Press, 1994).

Salzman, Marian, and Teresa Reisgies, *150 Ways Teens Can Make a Difference: A Handbook for Action* (Princeton, NJ: Peterson's Guides, 1991).

Schwartz, Linda, *What Do You Think? A Kid's Guide to Dealing with Daily Dilemmas* (Santa Barbara, CA: The Learning Works, 1993).
———*What Would You Do? A Kid's Guide to Tricky and Sticky Situations* (Santa Barbara, CA: The Learning Works, 1991).

The Values Library (New York: The Rosen Publishing Group, 1990–1993). Topics include responsibility, compassion, honesty, citizenship, self-esteem, tolerance, morality, cooperation, and more.

Resources from Search Institute

Through its Healthy Communities • Healthy Youth initiative, Search Institute offers many practical resources for building assets in youth and creating healthy communities. Selected titles include:

▶ *101 Asset-Building Actions* (full-color poster in English and Spanish)
▶ *150 Ways to Show Kids You Care* by Jolene L. Roehlkepartain
▶ *All Kids Are Our Kids* by Peter L. Benson

- ▶ *Assets: The Magazine of Ideas for Healthy Communities & Healthy Youth* (quarterly magazine)
- ▶ *Boxed In and Bored: How Middle Schools Continue to Fail Young Adolescents—and What Good Middle Schools Do Right* by Peter C. Scales
- ▶ *Building Assets in Congregations: A Practical Guide to Helping Youth Grow Up Healthy* by Eugene C. Roehlkepartain
- ▶ *Building Assets Together: 135 Group Activities for Helping Youth Succeed* by Jolene L. Roehlkepartain
- ▶ *Creating Intergenerational Community: 75 Ideas for Building Relationships Between Youth and Adults* by Jolene L. Roehlkepartain
- ▶ *A Foundation for Success: Congregations Building Assets in Youth* (25-minute video)
- ▶ *Healthy Communities • Healthy Youth* by Peter L. Benson and Eugene C. Roehlkepartain (booklet)
- ▶ *Learning and Living: How Asset Building for Youth Can Unify a School's Mission* by Donald Draayer and Eugene C. Roehlkepartain
- ▶ *Parenting with a Purpose: A Positive Approach for Raising Confident, Caring Youth* by Dean Feldmeyer and Eugene C. Roehlkepartain
- ▶ *Starting Out Right: Developmental Assets for Children* by Nancy Leffert, Peter L. Benson, and Jolene L. Roehlkepartain
- ▶ *Tapping the Potential: Discovering Congregations' Role in Building Assets in Youth* by Glenn A. Seefeldt and Eugene C. Roehlkepartain

To request a copy of our current catalog, contact us at:

Search Institute
615 First Avenue NE, Suite 125
Minneapolis, MN 55413
Toll-free telephone: 1-800-888-7828
In Minneapolis/St. Paul: (612) 376-8955
email: si@search-institute.org
www.search-institute.org

Resources from
Free Spirit Publishing

Founded in 1983, Free Spirit Publishing specializes in books and learning materials for kids, parents, and teachers. Many of our books address asset development. Selected titles include:

▶ *Bringing Up Parents: The Teenager's Handbook* by Alex J. Packer, Ph.D.

▶ *Bullies Are a Pain in the Brain*, written and illustrated by Trevor Romain

▶ *Fighting Invisible Tigers: A Stress Management Guide for Teens* by Earl Hipp (a Leader's Guide is available)

▶ *Growing Good Kids: 28 Activities to Enhance Self-Awareness, Compassion, and Leadership* by Deb Delisle and Jim Delisle, Ph.D.

▶ *How to Do Homework Without Throwing Up*, written and illustrated by Trevor Romain

▶ *How to Help Your Child with Homework: Every Caring Parent's Guide to Encouraging Good Study Habits and Ending the Homework Wars* by Marguerite C. Radencich, Ph.D., and Jeanne Shay Schumm, Ph.D.

▶ *I Like Being Me: Poems for Children About Feeling Special, Appreciating Others, and Getting Along* by Judy Lalli

▶ *Just Because I Am: A Child's Book of Affirmation* by Lauren Murphy Payne, M.S.W. (a Leader's Guide is available)

▶ *The Kid's Guide to Service Projects: Over 500 Service Ideas for Young People Who Want to Make a Difference* by Barbara A. Lewis

▶ *The Kid's Guide to Social Action: How to Solve the Social Problems You Choose—and Turn Creative Thinking into Positive Action* by Barbara A. Lewis

▶ *Kids with Courage: True Stories About Young People Making a Difference* by Barbara A. Lewis

▶ *Make Someone Smile and 40 More Ways to Be a Peaceful Person* by Judy Lalli

▶ *Making the Most of Today: Daily Readings for Young People on Self-Awareness, Creativity, and Self-Esteem* by Pamela Espeland and Rosemary Wallner

▶ *Raising Healthy Children Day by Day: 366 Readings for Parents, Teachers, and Caregivers, Birth to Age 5* by Jolene L. Roehlkepartain

▶ *School Power: Study Skill Strategies for Succeeding in School* by Jeanne Shay Schumm, Ph.D.

▶ *Stick Up for Yourself! Every Kid's Guide to Personal Power and Positive Self-Esteem* by Gershen Kaufman, Ph.D., Lev Raphael, Ph.D., and Pamela Espeland (a Teacher's Guide is available)

▶ *Taking Charge of My Mind & Body: A Girls' Guide to Outsmarting Alcohol, Drugs, Smoking, and Eating Problems* by Gladys Folkers, M.A., and Jeanne Engelmann

▶ *Talk with Teens About Feelings, Family, Relationships, and the Future: 50 Guided Discussions for School and Counseling Groups* by Jean Sunde Peterson, Ph.D.

▶ *Talk with Teens About Self and Stress: 50 Guided Discussions for School and Counseling Groups* by Jean Sunde Peterson, Ph.D.

▶ *We Can Get Along: A Child's Book of Choices* by Lauren Murphy Payne, M.S.W., and Claudia Rohling (a Leader's Guide is available)

▶ *What Do You Stand For? A Kid's Guide to Building Character* by Barbara A. Lewis

▶ *What Teens Need to Succeed: Proven, Practical Ways to Shape Your Own Future* by Peter L. Benson, Ph.D., Judy Galbraith, M.A., and Pamela Espeland

▶ *What Young Children Need to Succeed: Working Together to Build Assets from Birth to Age 11* by Jolene L. Roehlkepartain and Nancy Leffert, Ph.D.

To request a copy of our current catalog, contact us at:

Free Spirit Publishing Inc.
217 Fifth Avenue North, Suite 200
Minneapolis, MN 55401-1299
Toll-free telephone: 1-800-735-7323
In Minneapolis/St. Paul: (612) 338-2068
email: help4kids@freespirit.com
www.freespirit.com

Index

About the Authors

Peter L. Benson, Ph.D., has been president of Search Institute since 1985. He received his Ph.D. in social psychology from the University of Denver, his M.A. in psychology from Yale, and his B.A. in psychology from Augustana College. He is the author of several publications including *All Kids Are Our Kids: What Communities Must Do to Raise Caring and Responsible Children and Adolescents,* published by Jossey-Bass; *The Troubled Journey: A Portrait of 6th–12th Grade Youth,* published by Search Institute; and *The Quicksilver Years: The Hopes and Fears of Early Adolescence,* published by Harper & Row.

Judy Galbraith, M.A., is the founder and president of Free Spirit Publishing Inc. in Minneapolis, creators of SELF-HELP FOR KIDS® and SELF-HELP FOR TEENS® books and learning materials. A former classroom teacher, she received an education degree from the University of Wisconsin at Steven's Point and holds a master's degree in guidance and counseling of the gifted from Norwich University in Vermont. She is the author of *The Gifted Kids' Survival Guides* and coauthor of *When Gifted Kids Don't Have All the Answers,* published by Free Spirit.

Pamela Espeland has authored or coauthored many books for children and adults including *Life Lists for Teens: Tips, Steps, Hints, and How-Tos for Growing Up, Getting Along, Learning, and Having Fun; Making the Most of Today: Daily Readings for Young People on Self-Awareness, Creativity, and Self-Esteem;* and *Teach to Reach: Over 300 Strategies and Helpful Hints for Teachers of All Grades,* all published by Free Spirit. She graduated from Carleton College in Northfield, Minnesota.

Other Great Products from Free Spirit

What Teens Need to Succeed
Proven, Practical Ways to Shape
Your Own Future
*by Peter L. Benson, Ph.D.,
Judy Galbraith, M.A., and Pamela Espeland*
Based on a nationwide survey, this book
describes 40 developmental "assets"
all teens need to succeed in life, then
gives hundreds of suggestions teens
can use to build their own assets at home, at school, in the
community, in the congregation, with friends, and with youth
organizations. For ages 11 & up.
$15.95; 368 pp.; softcover; illus.; 7¼" x 9¼"

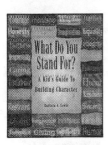

What Do You Stand For?
A Kid's Guide to Building Character
by Barbara A. Lewis
Young people need guidance from caring
adults to build strong, positive character
traits—but they can also build their own.
This inspiring book invites them to
explore and practice honesty, kindness,
empathy, integrity, tolerance, patience,
respect, and more. For ages 11 & up.
*$19.95; 284 pp.; softcover, illus.;
8½" x 11"*

What Do You Stand For? Poster
$9.95; 18" x 24"; full-color

What Do You Stand For?
Character Stickers
*$5.95; set of 96 stickers on 6
sheets (approx. 1" x 1¼"); full-color*

Stick With It! Magnets
*$19.95; set of 35 (one 3¾" x 3",
34 1" x 2"); full-color*

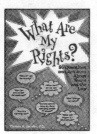

What Are My Rights?

95 Questions and Answers
About Teens and the Law

by Thomas A. Jacobs, J.D.

Teens need to know about the laws that affect them—so they can make informed decisions about what they should and shouldn't do. This fascinating book helps teens understand the law, recognize their responsibilities, and appreciate their rights. For ages 12 & up.

$14.95; 208 pp.; softcover; 6" x 9"

Stick Up for Yourself!

Every Kid's Guide to Personal Power and Positive Self-Esteem

Revised and Updated

by Gershen Kaufman, Ph.D., Lev Raphael, Ph.D., and Pamela Espeland

Simple text teaches assertiveness, responsibility, relationship skills, choice making, problem solving, and goal setting. For ages 8–12.

$11.95; 128 pp.; softcover; illus.; 6" x 9"

A Teacher's Guide to Stick Up for Yourself!

For teachers, grades 3–7.

$19.95; 128 pp.; softcover; 8½" x 11"

Bringing Up Parents

The Teenager's Handbook

by Alex J. Packer, Ph.D.

Straight talk and specific suggestions on how teens can talk to their parents so parents will listen, and how to take the initiative to resolve conflicts with parents, improve family relationships, earn trust, accept responsibility, and help to create a happier, healthier home environment. For ages 13 & up.

$15.95; 272 pp.; softcover; illus.; 7¼" x 9¼"

Visit us on the Web!

www.freespirit.com

Stop by anytime to find our Parents' Choice Approved catalog with fast, easy, secure 24-hour online ordering; "Ask Our Authors," where visitors ask questions—and authors give answers—on topics important to children, teens, parents, teachers, and others who care about kids; links to other Web sites we know and recommend; fun stuff for everyone, including quick tips and strategies from our books; and much more! Plus our site is completely searchable so you can find what you need in a hurry. Stop in and let us know what you think!

Just point and click!

 Get the first look at our books, catch the latest news from Free Spirit, and check out our site's newest features.

 Do you have a question for us or for one of our authors? Send us an email. Whenever possible, you'll receive a response within 48 hours.

 Order in confidence! Our secure server uses the most sophisticated online ordering technology available. And ordering online is just one of the ways to purchase our books: you can also order by phone, fax, or regular mail. No matter which method you choose, excellent service is our goal.

1.800.735.7323 • fax 612.337.5050 • help4kids@freespirit.com